Media Law

SAGE COURSE COMPANIONS
KNOWLEDGE AND SKILLS *for* SUCCESS

Media Law
Duncan Bloy

SAGE Publications

London ● Thousand Oaks ● New Delhi

First published 2006

SAGE Publications Ltd
1 Oliver's Yard
55 City Road
London EC1Y 1SP

SAGE Publications Inc.
2455 Teller Road
Thousand Oaks, California 91320

SAGE Publications India Pvt Ltd
B-42, Panchsheel Enclave
Post Box 4109
New Delhi 110 017

British Library Cataloguing in Publication data

A catalogue record for this book is available from the British Library

ISBN-10 1-4129-1119-2   ISBN-13 978-1-4129-1119-1
ISBN-10 1-4129-1120-6 (pbk)   ISBN-13 978-1-4129-1120-7 (pbk)

Library of Congress Control Number: 2006928577

Typeset by C&M Digitals (P) Ltd., Chennai, India
Printed on paper from sustainable resources
Printed in Great Britain by The Cromwell Press Ltd, Trowbridge, Wiltshire

contents

preface

If you have purchased this book, then you will probably be studying media law as a component of an undergraduate degree course in media studies or perhaps you are reading for a law degree and media law is an option that appeals to you. Alternatively, you may be a trainee journalist with aspirations to reach the top of your chosen profession and have concluded that to work within the law will certainly not hinder your progress in attaining that goal.

Prior to purchasing this book, you may have invested in one of a number of established works in the field of media law. Among the best-known ones are Geoffrey Robertson and Andrew Nicol's *Media Law* (Penguin, 2002), now in its fourth edition, and *MacNae's Law for Journalists*, by Tom Welsh, Walter Greenwood and David Banks (Oxford University Press, 2005), which has survived the test of time and, at the time of writing, is in its eighteenth edition. Both, in their respective ways, are informative, challenging and incisive. It will be apparent that lawyers have written the former primarily for those in or entering the legal profession and journalists (albeit with legal knowledge and training) have written the latter for aspiring scribes and broadcasters. *Media Law* runs to over 900 pages and *MacNae's Law for Journalists* to a tad under 600.

The critical question is, how does one deal with this abundance of information when faced with studying media law for the first time? This book seeks to address this problem. The Introduction explains the ethos of the series and the rationale underpinning this particular text. You will discover that the primary aim is to give informed advice on how to deal with the intricacies of the law in the context of conventional assessment regimes. You are likely to be faced with both coursework and formal examination as part of the assessment process. An examination may take many forms, including unseen, open-book, take home and multiple choice. The type of coursework to be faced will, in all probability, depend on whether you are an undergraduate or in training to become a journalist. The former is likely to demand a critical analysis of a particular aspect or aspects of the law. For trainee journalists, at the very least, two things will be expected. The first is an *explanation* of the relevant legal principles and the second will seek to find out what the journalists believe *should* or *can be* published or broadcast, given the legal context in which they are operating. The legal context will invariably, but not inevitably, seek to place some restraints on the freedom of expression that journalists value so highly.

The Introduction also emphasises the importance of making maximum use of *primary sources*. 'Primary sources', in the legal context, are legislation, statutory instruments and, crucially, court judgments. It is suggested that if these materials are accessed prior to reading journal articles and standard textbooks, then what is being discussed in these publications will be easier to comprehend. Examiners will always give credit to students who can demonstrate a precise knowledge of primary source material.

To utilise primary sources to the maximum suggests ready access to a quality law library. However, this is no longer a necessary prerequisite as far as statutory material and case law are concerned. In the Introduction I will show you how these features can be readily accessed by anyone who has an Internet connection (preferably broadband) and a PC linked to a printer. Visits to law libraries for those with such facilities are therefore likely to be reduced and only undertaken to access journals or books.

Part One seeks to persuade you to adopt a positive approach to learning. At this stage of your education or training you are unlikely to be able to approach a legal problem with the trained eye of a practising lawyer or an experienced journalist. However, your task is to begin to acquire the thinking processes associated with subject matter that depends heavily on analytical and interpretative skills. The journalist will turn to the media lawyer in order to discover whether a particular story can be published without fear of being sued or will, in fact, lead to its author being found to be in contempt of court. Journalists and broadcasters should have a working knowledge of the legal context in which they are operating, but it takes the lawyers – and, ultimately, the judges – to determine whether or not they are indeed acting lawfully in carrying out their functions.

Part One will introduce a number of 'overriding principles' that journalists seek to rely on to justify publication. More about this later, but it will do no harm to mention two key elements at this stage. The first is the Human Rights Act 1998 and, with it, the introduction into English law of Article 10 of the European Convention on Human Rights. Article 10 deals with *freedom of expression*. The second is the concept of the *public interest*.

Part Two makes direct reference to the content of the curriculum with which you are likely to be faced. This section is, of necessity, the core element of the book. There are major themes running throughout any media law syllabus. It should come as no surprise to discover that *defamation* is a major subject for discussion. Other major topics are *contempt of court, reporting restrictions, privacy* and *confidentiality, protection of journalists' sources and materials*, elements of *intellectual property law* and *media regulation* via bodies such as the Press Complaints Commission and the Office of Communications (Ofcom), established by the Communications Act 2003. It is a reasonable expectation that, with the bringing into force on 1 January 2005 of the Freedom of Information Act 2000, this topic will also figure in examinations in the foreseeable future. Another 'growth area' is online journalism and, consequently, the increasing potential for libel via the Internet. Of particular interest is the question, from which jurisdictions may remedies be sought? You must bear in mind, however, that the media spawns an enormous amount of litigation and a major task is for me to show you:

- how to keep up to date
- how to ensure that you gain maximum benefit from the latest case law developments.

Part Three is what might be referred to as a *technical* section. It aims to provide you with the relevant study and revision skills to help you attain the highest marks possible. I must admit that I believe discussing study skills in a generic sense is not particularly helpful. By the time a person enters university, he or she will usually have a study system worked out. It is difficult to persuade people to make fundamental changes if their approach to study has already reaped rewards. In this part of the book, therefore, I will explain how to identify your studying technique's strengths and weaknesses and how, where appropriate, to modify your approach to meet the expectations of tutors in this subject. Elsewhere, in Part Three, I will give you pointers on what your tutors will be looking for when they come to set assessment questions or coursework. I will also emphasise the importance of thinking and writing logically and coherently. Written answers – whether essays or examination answers – require you to commence with an introduction, address the issues raised and provide a conclusion.

The final part comprises notes on a significant number of important cases that have helped to shape the way media law operates. The majority are from England and Wales, but there are also notes on important decisions of the European Court of Human Rights. The facts of each case are reduced to a bare minimum and the note on each decision aims to provide you with the major reason for that decision and, where relevant, the implications of the judgment. Clearly, given the limitations on the space available, these case notes are not meant to replace consideration of the actual reports. They should be able to help with your revision, though, in the sense that you will be able to identify the major points that have come from each case.

It is incumbent on you to take on board the messages flagged up in the various parts of this book. However, unlike some areas of legal study, this subject should not be approached in an overly academic way. The law cannot be divorced from the practice of journalism and broadcasting. The law appears to encourage a free press and that is consistent with the aims of a healthy democracy. However, the law will, on occasion, seek to apply restraints to the way the media operates. As a media law student, you will have to seek to assess the demands of a free press in relation to other interests, such as an individual's reputation, and offer reasons for which you believe should prevail in a given set of circumstances. This book is designed to help you to come to the right conclusions.

acknowledgements

This book is primarily designed to assist undergraduate students in achieving success in the varying assessment regimes that one finds in university law and media schools. It was not designed with the NCTJ law examinations in mind, although students sitting those examinations may glean some assistance from the book's legal content.

On the 5 October 2006 the House of Lords delivered a significant judgment in the case of *Jameel v. Wall Street Journal (Europe) Ltd [2006] UKHL 44*. I would like to express my appreciation to the publishers for permitting me to include a resumé of the decision at the 11th hour in the publishing process. References in the text to the law on common law qualified privilege and the case of *Reynolds v. Times Newspapers* [1999] should now be read in light of this decision. Fortunately, the key principles remain the same. However the *approach* adopted by the judges when assessing whether the media can avail itself of the defence of Reynolds privilege is likely to be far more liberal than that demonstrated over the last five years or so.

I would also like to put readers on notice of vitally important decisions pending from the Court of Appeal. The *McKennitt v. Ash* appeal is to be heard in late November 2006 with a decision expected in January 2007. The court will have the benefit of written submissions on behalf of the media, such is the concern from both the print and broadcast media over the possible impact of the decision on the way the tabloid press and 'celebrity' magazines operate. Please read the sections in this book on privacy and confidentiality in light of the Court of Appeal decision. The Court of Appeal is also to consider the legal issues arising from the *Ackroyd* case dealing with protection of sources. Please watch out for this decision and take it into account when dealing with section 10 of the Contempt of Court Act 1981.

On a personal note I would like to express my gratitude to the editorial staff at Sage for their collective endeavours to bring the project to fruition in as short a time as possible. I would also like to thank my wife Lynda for her understanding as to why I wanted to write this particular text having told her two years ago that I 'wasn't going to do any more books.'

I have endeavoured to apply the law as I understood it as at 31 October 2006.

Duncan Bloy
Cardiff
November 2006

case list

case references

EWHC = England and Wales High Court
(QB = Queens Bench Division)
(Fam = Family Division)
(Admin = Administrative Division)
(Ch = Chancery Division)

EWCA = England and Wales Court of Appeal

(Civ = Civil Division)

All ER = All England Reports

e.g. [2005] 3 All ER 123 = Third volume for 2005 at page 123

AC = Appeal Cases

Decisions of the House of Lords. For example [1991] AC 1 = Appeal cases for 1991 at page 1. There being only one volume that year.

UKHL = United Kingdom House of Lords

The notation for House of Lords decisions found at either: www.parliament.uk or www.bailii.org websites

ECHR = European Human Rights Decisions

Go to www.echr.coe.int and follow the links to case law.

EMLR = Entertainment and Media Law Reports

e.g. [1994] EMLR 1 = First page of the volume for 1994.

FSR= Fleet Street Reports

Cr App Rep = Criminal Appeal Reports

e.g. [2001] 1 Cr App Rep = First volume of the Criminal Appeal Reports for 2001.

WLR = Weekly Law Reports

e.g. [2006] 2 WLR 123 = second volume of the Weekly Law Reports for 2006 at page 123.

Crim LR = Criminal Law Review

e.g. (2000) Crim LR 534 = Criminal Law Review for 2000 at page 534

ER = English Reports

Historical series. e.g. 64 ER 234 = 64th volume of the English Reports at page 234

EHHR = European Human Rights Reports

UKPC = United Kingdom Privy Council

Case reports available via www.baiili.org

CLR = Commonwealth Reports

Australian Law Report series

NZCA = New Zealand Court of Appeal Reports

US = United States Supreme Court Decisions

QB and KB = Queens Bench and King's Bench Reports

Part of the Official Law Reports Series.

IMPORTANT

The vast majority of case reports (full transcripts) that you are likely to need to consult are available on one of the following websites:

www.baiilli.org (British & Irish Legal Information Institute)

www.echr.coe.int (European Court of Human Rights)

www.5rb.co.uk (5 Raymond Buildings: Barristers' Chambers)

---

statutes

Access to Justice Act 1999 89
Administration of Justice
    Act 1960
    s. 12 89, 90

Broadcasting Act 1990 63, 138
Broadcasting Act 1996 52
Broadcasting Act 2001
    s. 10(3) 149

Children and Young Person's
    Act 1933 37, 138
    s. 39 86,87, 183

    s. 49 84,85
    s. 49(4A) 84
Children's Act 1989
    s. 97(2) 89, 90–91
Communications Act 2003 51.
Contempt of Court Act (CCA)
    1981 37, 47, 83, 99, 100, 103,
    106, 138
    s. 2 92, 93
    s. 2(2) 93, 94, 95, 99
    s. 2(3) 92
    s. 4 98
    s. 4(2) 47, 83, 92, 94, 98

Statutory instruments

European instruments

Let me set out as clearly as possible the intentions behind the Course Companions series as they apply to media law. The major aim is to assist you in achieving the highest possible marks in your assessment as a result of studying in a constructive and productive manner. In order to do this, you have to accept that this guide is not designed to replace the standard learning material provided by your tutors or lecturers. You must therefore regard this text as being supplementary to the reference material provided for your course. Hopefully, it will also encourage you to widen your reading and undertake greater research.

I am sure that most of you will have been provided at the outset of your course with some form of study guide. If so, please look at it now. It should detail which are the recommended textbooks for the course. One or more of the following are likely to appear:

- Robertson, G. and Nicol, A. (2002) *Media Law*, 4th edition, Penguin.
- Carey, P. and Sanders, J. (2004) *Media Law*, 3rd edition, Sweet & Maxwell.
- Crone, T. et al. (2002) *Law and the Media*, 4th edition, Focal Press.
- Welsh, T., Greenwood, W. and Banks, D. (2005) *McNae's Essential Law for Journalists*, 18th edition, Oxford University Press.

For good measure, your tutor may also have added to the list a 'cases and materials' book, although this is likely to have been done with some trepidation. This is because the courts tend to be highly productive in this area of law, with new and influential decisions being handed down on a regular basis and, thus, casebooks become dated very quickly. Throw into the melting pot an ever-increasing number of European Court of Human Rights decisions regarding the media and one can see why there are so few case books in existence for this subject. The book *Media Law Cases and Materials* by Eric Barendt and Lesley Hutchins (Longman, 2000) contains excellent material, but much of it is now of largely historic significance – and that despite the book being published only five years ago at the time of writing!

I'm sure you will agree that there is plenty of material to warrant your attention. Before we move on, think about the assessment regime that is also likely to be referred to in the guide. In all probability, you will have an unseen examination of between two and three hours and a coursework component, usually along the lines of a 2,000-word essay. The key question, therefore, is, 'How much of the law contained in those textbook pages will I need to know in order to excel in the assessment?' It is unrealistic to expect you to remember massive amounts of law relating to each component of the course, so you must ask yourself, 'Which, of all this material, is it critical that I understand?'

In order to answer that question, you must try to place yourself in the position of your tutor. Most tutors will want to demonstrate that the generally accepted 'core' components of the subject, mentioned in the Preface, are included for study. My guess is that, at the outset, you will be asked to consider certain conceptual elements relating to the way the media operates. Even ethics may warrant passing reference! This is likely to include a discussion about the importance of freedom of speech and the application of the principles enshrined in the European Convention on Human Rights. The major principles that we will discuss later in this book are *freedom of expression* (Article 10) and *the right to respect for private life* (Article 8). There may be some discussion at the outset about so-called enshrined rights by reference to written constitutions, such as that of the USA. This poses the question, 'Are some rights deemed to be more important than others?' You are therefore being asked to consider if the media's reliance on freedom of expression as a justification for publication should be regarded as omnipotent.

You may then be advised to look at key decisions from other jurisdictions for comparative purposes. Without pre-empting anything that may be said in Part Two, the sooner you are able to identify what I call five star case law the better. These are cases that your tutor will expect you to refer to when answering questions on particular topics. Therefore, right at the outset, make a decision to list all those cases that you believe will need to be cited in order to accumulate marks in the assessment process. For those of you not undertaking law degrees, the courts work on a hierarchical basis. The highest court in the land is the House of Lords and, therefore, a decision of the House is something that must be respected by lower courts. Your study guide will probably include an outline court structure and lists of cases relating to each topic under consideration. As a matter of good practice, try to categorise the list into those cases that must be cited, those that may need to be cited and those that are purely *illustrative*. This book will advise on how this can be achieved.

One cannot consider elements of media law in this country without looking at the parallel European jurisprudence relating to the interpretation of the European Convention on Human Rights. Take, for example, the highly publicised decision of the High Court in the *Galloway MP v. Telegraph Group Ltd [2004] EWHC 2786 (QB)* libel action. During the course of the trial, the European Court of Human Rights delivered its decision in the case of *Selistö v. Finland [2005] EMLR 178*, in which the court analysed Article 10 of the Convention in some detail. In the High Court, the judge, Mr Justice Eady, referred to the case in his judgment and considered the impact of the decision on whether or not the defence of qualified privilege pleaded by *The Telegraph* should succeed. Therefore, you may find it possible to group English and European cases that are linked – always, of course, indicating their importance. It will have been made clear that, when discussing legal issues, the reasoning underpinning a decision must be explained. One doesn't simply look at the report of a decision without asking the question 'Why did the court decide in *this* way as opposed to accepting a *different* point of view?'

Important and recent case law for England and Wales can easily be accessed at the British and Irish Legal Information Institutes website (at www.bailii.org).

Access the site's home page where you will see on the left hand side of the screen the words: **BAILII Cases and Legislation**. Underneath are listed the various jurisidiction: England and Wales, Ireland, Northern Ireland, Scotland etc. Click on 'England and Wales.' This will then take you to a list of all the courts in the jurisdiction of High Court Queens Bench cases. Click on the court you wish to access and the next screen will show the following:

- A search facility
- The alphabet
- A list of years

You now have a choice. You may enter the name of the case you wish to read into the search engine in order to locate its position. Second, you may press the letter of the alphabet that corresponds to the first letter of the name of the case. Third, if you know the year you can insert that and a full list of all cases for the year will be screened on a month by month basis. Once you have located the case click on the name and the full text will apper.

I mentioned above the impact of the European Court's decisions. The full text of these may be found on the European Court of Human Rights' website (at www.echr.coe.int). You must refer to Section 12 of the Human Rights Act 1998 to understand the context that explains why the European Court's decisions cannot be ignored. That section deals with freedom of expression. It states that, when a court is considering whether or not to grant relief and, if granted, the relief might *affect the exercising* of the right to freedom of expression, then 'the court must have particular regard to the importance of the Convention right to freedom of expression'. It is highly likely that you will have to make this point when answering questions – particularly problem questions – relating to issues affecting free expression. Note that the section uses the word 'particular' to qualify the word 'regard.' You must, therefore, enquire if this means, in effect, that judges must make reference to the provision in their decision making in relevant cases. In other words, they are not entitled simply to pay lip-service to the provision.

Another point to emphasise at the outset is the importance of coming to terms with legislative provisions, the interpretation and construction of which provide the reason for being in the court in the first place. All public general statutes from 1988 onwards are to be found in full text form at the website of the Office of Public Sector Information (at www.opsi.gov.uk) and this means that virtually all the legislation that is relevant to your course can be found online, without the need to visit a law library. No one would pretend that reading statutes is exhilarating, but it is vital that you make yourself familiar with the particular sections or words within a section that have attracted judicial attention. The easy and relatively more interesting way to do this is to check on the following.

- Each statute has a *short title* that will inform you of the underlying purpose of the legislation. For example, the short title for the Human Rights Act 1998 is stated thus:

  An Act to give further effect to rights and freedoms guaranteed under the European Convention on Human Rights; to make provision with respect to holders of certain judicial offices who become judges of the European Court of Human Rights; and for connected purposes.

- If you utilise the OPSI's website (address given above), you will be able to access *explanatory notes* for each piece of legislation from 1999 onwards, which seek to put each part of every Act into context.
- For each section, there is a marginal note indicating the purpose of the section. For example, section 1 of the Human Rights Act has the side note

'The Convention Rights' and these are then stated to be Articles 2–12 and 14 of the European Convention on Human Rights. The section continues by identifying certain Articles from the first and sixth protocols.

In Part One, I will illustrate this with an example from the House of Lords decision of *Cream Holdings Ltd & Others v. Banerjee & Others [2004] UKHL 44.*

Students often endeavour to read a case report, textbook or journal article without fully appreciating the statutory context. This is a big mistake! What is being said is far more likely to make sense if you are aware of the word, or words, at the heart of a controversy. Please remember that a judge may be asked to decide the meaning of a single word. In the Queen's Bench Divisional Court in late 2004, the judges in the case of *Zafar v. Director of Public Prosecutions [2004] EWHC2468 (QB)* had to decide the meaning of the word 'breath' in the context of section 5 of the Road Traffic Act 1988. The word 'breath' may appear to be a simple one to construe, but the issue for the court was whether or not Parliament, when using the word in the Act, meant it to refer to 'deep lung air' only! The point that I am trying to make is that reading the decision in this case or any comments on it would be relatively futile without first being aware of the words in Section 5 of the Act, together with knowledge of the *purpose* of the legislation. The purpose, clearly, is to discourage people from driving having consumed excess alcohol.

Your lecturers will expect you to cite, where appropriate, journal articles as part of any analytical answer to a problem. There are several highly respected legal journals, such as the *Law Quarterly Review* and the *Modern Law Review.* These journals carry articles on many different legal topics, including media law. The major 'dedicated' journal is the *Entertainment Law Review,* published by Sweet & Maxwell eight times per year. The *Review* does not simply focus on UK law and so, at times, you will find articles that have no particular relevance to your level of study. Nevertheless, you need to check out its contents on a regular basis. Your tutor or lecturer should draw your attention to recently published articles. They tend to be generated as a result of legislative change, the need for legislative intervention or important judicial decisions. Given the contemporary nature of decision making, an extremely useful source of comment for the busy student is to be found on the websites of media law specialists – either firms of solicitors or barristers' chambers. The following are good sources of information:

- www.5rb.co.uk
- www.onebrickcourt.com
- www.carter-ruck.com

The above list is simply indicative of the high-quality legal comment that is available from such sources. Another way to access these sources is simply to enter the name of a case into a standard search engine, such as Google or Yahoo!, and numerous web sources will be listed. It is then up to you to choose which are the most appropriate for your needs.

Most university libraries will subscribe to the *Entertainment and Media Law Reports*. Published by Sweet & Maxwell, they are the only dedicated set of reports dealing with this area of law. The series was launched in 1993 and is regularly cited in courts. You will be referred to cases appearing in them and should therefore consult the reports regularly. Do remember, though, that many, if not the majority, of these cases will also be available on the www.bailii.org and/or the www.5rb.co.uk websites and, therefore, readily accessible from home.

Other sources of information, which also offer potential for research, are official reports or reports of inquiries such as the Hutton Inquiry in 2004 (this report can be found at www.the-hutton-inquiry.org.uk). This report will give you a unique insight into how the media works with its *sources* and the lengths to which journalists will go to protect the identities of their sources.

Preparing for coursework will often require different skills from those used when working or revising for examinations. There will be an expectation that you have undertaken a reasonable amount of research in preparation for producing an informed and well-argued piece of work. Coursework will often focus on one particular topic.

The law (or lack of) relating to privacy is often a topic on which an assessment essay is based. A little research into the subject will result in you ascertaining that there are recent publications devoted purely to this topic. Finding one up-to-date resource, such as Joshua Rozenburg's *Privacy and the Press* (Oxford University Press, 2004), will lead you, in this instance, to a bibliography of some 22 sources, all connected with the topic under review. Flick over the page and you will then discover a comprehensive list of cases, extending to four pages, all relevant to the law on privacy and confidentiality, albeit some more important than others. However, bear in mind that this book was published in 2004 before the leading cases of *Campbell v. MGN Ltd [2004] UKHL 22* and *Von Hannover v. Germany [2004]* EMLR 379 and the subsequent UK court decisions in 2005 and 2006 (see Parts One, Two and Four). This illustrates the point that things move on quickly in media law. Further information on privacy can be gleaned from the 5th Report of session 2002–3 of the House of Commons Culture, Media and Sport Committee, published in June 2003. This report, entitled *Privacy and*

Media Intrusion, contains a wealth of information, opinion and comment regarding the interrelationship between the media's search for news and the desire of individuals to keep elements of their lives out of the public gaze. This report spawned a reasonably rapid (albeit negative) response from government in October 2003 (this can be accessed at www. publications. parliament.uk).

I hope the above introduction has given you a basic insight into how to proceed with your studies in media law. Those of you studying for a law degree may be familiar with how the courts work, but should still take on board the need for adopting an informed approach to the material facing you. The expectations of tutors on journalism training courses and media degrees may be slightly different than those on law degrees, but nevertheless, all these students will be dealing with the same material and need to ensure that they are not overwhelmed by its sheer volume. In the next part of this book I will put tutors' expectations in context and explain how best you can meet those expectations when progressing through your course.

part one

media law: the basics

- Thinking like a lawyer?
- Categorisation
- Themes
- Thinking like a journalist
- Conclusion

1.1
thinking like a lawyer?

My task in this part of the book is to persuade you to think like a lawyer or, to be more precise, like a media lawyer. The way in which a lawyer operates varies little from subject to subject – the approach to the law remaining virtually the same, irrespective of subject content. However, the challenge for me is to also give advice to those who have no wish to become lawyers. Those who are enrolled on media studies degrees or training to become journalists will have to respond to differing expectations from their tutors. What follows, therefore, is an attempt to identify generic issues pertinent to all groups of students irrespective of course. From there, I will consider areas of divergence in order to meet the different expectations of course tutors.

All students then will be expected to *deal* with the law. This requires an appreciation of the legal environment in which the media operates and an understanding of varying elements of the English legal system. Let's deal with the latter aspect first.

Most of our law is created by Parliament and it is often stated that we live in a parliamentary democracy. We are deemed to subscribe to the rule of law. Parliament is not only responsible for creating *primary legislation* – that is, Acts of Parliament – but also *secondary legislation*, in the form of statutory instruments. Primary legislation can be wide-ranging and lacking in specific detail. Statutory instruments issued at various times after the legislation has received royal assent will bring particular provisions into force and may also provide further rules about how a section is to operate. The principle behind this approach is supportable, but, in practice, difficulties can be caused. The first question a student has to ask about any piece of legislation is 'Have all its provisions been brought into force?' You will lose marks if you assume that a section of an act is in force just because the act has received royal assent. Let me give an example relevant to media law.

In 1999, Parliament created the Youth Justice and Criminal Evidence Act. A cursory look at the statute shows that there are three parts and some 68 sections, not counting various schedules. The only part of real interest to media law and journalism students is Part Two, Chapter IV, dealing with reporting restrictions. Let no one doubt, they are important provisions and impact on the ability of journalists to report the courts in a fair and accurate way. Since 1999, students have been asking, 'Which, if any, of these sections in Chapter IV are actually in force?' The answer was that none of them was in force until 7 October 2004, when section 46, part of Section 48 and part of Schedule 2 came into force. Courts now have the power to prevent the press from publishing anything that will reveal the identity of a witness if it is satisfied that the witness is 'vulnerable'. In effect, 'this means that the quality of the evidence or the witness' level of cooperation will be diminished by fear or distress and that the situation will be improved by an order being made.

> *Please ensure that you know whether a section or sections of an Act of Parliament are in force at the time of writing, otherwise you will suffer embarrassment and loss of credit. Tutors expect your knowledge to be up to date.*

From even a cursory look at a piece of legislation, you will have gleaned that, despite the best endeavours of the Plain English Campaign, those who draft it are not always on message. Every person in the jurisdiction is expected to know the law. However, even the simplest English word can cause problems of interpretation. Therefore, when there is a dispute over the meaning of words, the judges are called on to decide which is the correct interpretation. The ostensibly simple question they have to answer is what was Parliament's intention when it used the words in the statute?

In very simplistic terms, in a courtroom, the judges will receive 'advice' from barristers representing the 'warring' factions. Barristers, despite their allegiance to their clients, are meant to 'assist' a judge in coming to the correct conclusion. In an endeavour to ensure consistency of approach, English law relies on the concept of *precedent*. The barristers will therefore trawl through past decisions of courts and base their arguments either on the precedents or argue that past decisions should not apply to the current situation. Your function when thinking like a lawyer is to first put yourself in the position of the barristers for each side and work out the basis of the respective arguments. Then you must assume the role of the judge and decide between the competing views. Critically, a judge must give reasons for the decision and, likewise, in an examination, you must also give reasons for reaching your conclusion.

Always try to look at a legal problem from both sides, even though you may have been asked to advise one side or the other. Remember also that you must give reasons for your decision. When reading cases, always ask yourself the question, 'Why did the court decide as it did?'

Before you can do yourself justice in this process, you must identify what actually is the problem. This means that you must look at the wording of a particular section of an Act of Parliament under investigation. Is it one word or a series of words that are causing problems in construction? You should then ask yourself, 'Is there any assistance that you can call on to help decide the correct interpretation?' Law students everywhere should be familiar with the decision of the House of Lords in *Pepper v. Hart [1993] 1 All ER 42*. Its importance here is as authority for the proposition that judges can look at parliamentary material, such as *Hansard,* as an aid to construction of statutes. Until this case, judges were prevented from accessing such sources and had to rely only on the words used in the act. In this case, the House of Lords emphasised the *purposive* approach to the construction of legislation – a point that you might wish to make in your assessment.

Remember that you can look beyond the words of an act in order to assist in determining the correct construction to be placed on a contentious word or phrase.

We now come to the important doctrine of *precedent*. When analysing an examination problem, you will become aware of this subject area. Is this a question regarding defamation or reporting restrictions or journalist's sources? Based on the information provided in your study guide or on your tutorial sheets, you will be able to identify a number of cases relating to the area under discussion. The cases will fit both into a broad category and a subcategory. For example, the 'broad category' may be *defamation* and the 'subcategory' could be *prior restraint*. Having done this with the cases, you then need to use a system to remind you of the importance of each case. I recommend you use a star system, with five being 'vital' down to one, which might be described as 'illustrative'. Your tutors will expect you to cite case law authority when undertaking your analysis. They will also expect greater knowledge of and reliance on a five-star case than on a one-star case. I will illustrate this a little later on when we look at the *Cream Holdings* case.

Become familiar with the importance of the doctrine of precedent. It enables you to act like a lawyer when citing cases and discussing their relative merits and strengths (and weaknesses) in relation to the problem under discussion. Start this process at the outset of your studies and appreciate that the lists you create make an ongoing contribution to revision.

The next question you might ask is 'How am I expected to write about case law?' The critical point is, of course, the decision. In order to start accumulating marks, you must give a correct synopsis of the decision. By way of explanation and example, let me take the case of *Armstrong v. Times Newspapers,* decided by the High Court in late December 2004. The brief facts of the case are that, at the time, Lance Armstrong was a famous cyclist who alleged that an article in *The Sunday Times* defamed him, in that it suggested he took performance-enhancing drugs or that there were reasonable grounds to suspect that he took such drugs. *The Sunday Times* pleaded qualified privilege and justification as its defences. The judge rejected qualified privilege for the reason mentioned above – that is, the newspaper had acted irresponsibly in not giving him an adequate chance to put his side of the argument or refute the allegations. If you were writing about the *Armstrong* case, it would probably read something like this:

In the case of Armstrong v. Times Newspapers Ltd [2004] EWHC 2928 (QB), *Eady J decided that the newspaper could not rely on the defence of qualified privilege.*

That is a correct statement of fact and perhaps warrants one mark.

However, it will be clear that no reason has been stated for *why* the judge reached that conclusion. To accumulate more marks, the better student would continue along the following lines:

In reaching this conclusion, the judge took into account the well-established duty/interest test, or, the right to know test, as described by the House of Lords in Reynolds v. Times Newspapers Ltd [1999] UKHL 45 *and endorsed by the Court of Appeal in* Loutchansky v. Times Newspapers [2001].

At this point, you are scoring well because you have mentioned a key test and also cited important case law to show the 'authority' of the test. If you have already dealt with the defences to defamation actions on your course, you will be aware that Reynolds is a five-star case and Loutchansky is not far behind.

Yet, the good student will not be satisfied with concluding at that point because the reasoning behind the decision is absent. Therefore, something along the lines of the following is needed (note that the numbers in brackets relate to comments on the points, which are given below):

> *A major element (1) when considering the application of the duty-interest test (2) is to ask whether or not the newspaper could be said to be under a duty to publish these allegations about this claimant at that time. (3) The judge decided that it was not under such a duty 'without affording him an opportunity of giving a measured response to the charges'. (4) The judge appears to be reiterating the point made in* Galloway MP v. *(5)* Telegraph Group Ltd (2004) EWHC 2786 (QB) *in order to rely on the defence of qualified privilege, the newspaper must act in accordance with the factors supporting the concept of responsible journalism (6) identified by Lord Nicholls (7) in* Reynolds. *(8) As a result of the* Galloway *and* Armstrong *cases, it would appear that, where a person's reputation is at stake, the courts are increasingly likely to conclude that the claimant should be given an adequate opportunity to comment on the allegation the newspaper is bringing into the public domain. Failure to do so will result in the comprehensive defence of qualified privilege being denied to the defendants. (9)*

Comments: These numbers relate to the points made in the example of an answer given above.

1 Good point. The good student shows the examiner he or she is aware that what is being stated is an important legal point.

2 Good point. The student shows the examiner that he or she is about to comment on the key test.

3 Good points. The major question is not simply whether or not this is a public interest story but also if these allegations should have been made at that time about this person. Here the good student is demonstrating that he or she has read the report and is aware of the words used by the judge.

4 Good point. This shows that the student is aware that a fundamental principle of good journalism is a that story should have 'balance.'

5 Good point. By mentioning the *Galloway* case, decided by the same judge only two weeks before the *Armstrong* decision, the student shows that he or she is up to date with case law.

6 Good point. The *Reynolds* case endorsed a number of factors that were to be taken into account when deciding whether or not a newspaper had acted responsibly. The good student, shows that he or she knows this important point.

7 Good point. Lord Nicholls in *Reynolds* identified the factors mentioned in (6) above. It adds polish to the answer to be able to mention this fact.

8 Good point. The student demonstrates that he or she understands the significance of the *Reynolds* case.

9 Excellent. The student now uses his or her own words to draw the examiner's attention to the conclusion drawn from the *Armstrong* and *Galloway* cases. Students who can manage to avoid simple description and indulge in some critical or analytical thinking will usually be rewarded with high grades.

The good student will also have noted that a single judge in the High Court has decided the *Armstrong* case and therefore the decision is not as authoritative as, say, one from the Court of Appeal or the House of Lords. The student will therefore be expected to justify reliance on this case. This can be done in a number of ways. Perhaps the strongest argument is that the case is the most recent example of judicial decision making as far as the defence of qualified privilege is concerned. A second argument is that the judge is relying on and applying the principles contained in *Reynolds v. Times Newspapers Ltd,* the leading case in this area of law. A third argument you could employ is that Mr Justice Eady is a very experienced judge who specialises in defamation law and, therefore, his reasoning should be given respect.

I hope the above analysis has given you an insight into what is likely to be expected from your tutors, particularly when you have been asked to analyse a series of facts containing a small number of legal issues.

Another significant point about the *Armstrong* and *Galloway* cases is that the judge considers each of the ten *Reynolds* factors (see p. 185) or criteria relating to 'responsible journalism' (more about this in Part Two).

Students often ask if they need to give a full reference when citing cases, as is the usual practice in a court. The answer is no. Most lecturers would not wish you to waste time trying to remember the date and reference to a case. You might choose to put the date in brackets after you first mention a case in an examination answer, but you would only do that in order to show that it is a recent decision and may represent the latest thinking on a particular area of law. However, do be careful. If you are not sure of the date, omit it. To write *Reynolds [1979]* as opposed to the correct date of 1999 could force the examiner to wonder if you really do understand the historical significance of the case. In this respect, *Reynolds* is important because it was the first case to be decided *after* the Human Rights Act 1998 went on to the statute book but *before* it was brought into effect, on 2 October 2000.

The point has been made earlier that lawyers do cite court cases from jurisdictions other than England and Wales. The basic principle is that decisions of higher courts in this jurisdiction are binding on lower courts – hence the term *binding precedent*. Judges have to *follow* their reasoning the same way in order to maintain a high degree of consistency in the application of the law. In theory, citizens need to at least know what the law is so that they can decide what actions to take or refrain from taking. The assumption, therefore, is that decisions from other jurisdictions are not binding on courts in this jurisdiction. Nevertheless, the same issue that is being examined by an English court may already have been dealt with in another jurisdiction. Arguably, it would be foolhardy to not take account of the reasoning of the overseas court. These decisions are said to have *persuasive* authority in this jurisdiction. Most notably, judges might be persuaded by decisions in commonwealth countries because they have a legacy of English common law in their court systems. In the days when Britain had an Empire, final appeals used to be sent to London to be heard by the Privy Council. This body still exists today and comprises members of the Judicial Committee of the House of Lords. Its jurisdiction is severely limited these days because only a small number of former colonies regard the Privy Council as the final court of appeal. The majority of these countries are former colonies in the West Indies, such as Jamaica and Trinidad and Tobago, but, perhaps surprisingly, New Zealand still sends cases to be heard by the Privy Council. For detailed information about the work of the Privy Council and full text reports of its decisions since 1999, go to www.privy-council.org.uk and click on 'Judgments'.

In effect, therefore, we are dealing with two types of judgments – the first being the decisions from overseas jurisdictions and the second being cases decided by the Privy Council. Both may be taken into account, but, one might argue, the Privy Council's decisions are likely to be more influential because of the judicial composition of its Board. You will gain credit if you can draw the examiner's attention to the impact of some overseas decisions. As you progress through your course, simply list those persuasive decisions you believe have had an impact on the way the law has developed in this country. Let me give some examples of how such persuasive cases have been used.

The first relates to an area of law that one might label 'developing' – that of Internet libel. A leading authority is the Court of Appeal decision in *Lennox Lewis & Others v. Don King [2004] EWCA 1329*. This case is important because it was the *first* Court of Appeal decision to lay down the general principles of law to be applied. At the heart of the case is the question, 'In which jurisdiction may a claimant who believes he has been defamed as a result of information contained on a website sue?' It may seem like a strange question, but, if you look at the facts of this case, you will understand its significance.

The Internet transcends jurisdictional boundaries. In this case, the well-known boxing promoter, Don King – a citizen of the USA, with his home in Florida – alleged that he had been defamed as a result of two articles placed on websites based in California. The articles were placed on the websites by Judd Burstein, a New York lawyer representing Lennox Lewis and his production company, Lion Promotions, who had been in dispute with Don King. King pleaded that the words used meant that he (King) '… is a persistent, bigoted, and unashamed or unrepentant anti-Semite.' (It should be noted that the action was commenced against Lewis and Lion on the basis that Burstein was working for them, so they were 'responsible' for the comments. However, by the time the case reached the Court of Appeal, the action against Lewis and Lion had been discontinued on terms agreed between the parties.) So, in summary, we have a New York lawyer placing statements on a Californian website relating to a citizen of the USA who wishes to litigate in London! Now it is clear that in such a case literally anyone in the world can access the websites in question and, logically, if the person allegedly defamed has his or her reputation damaged within that country, then he or she ought to be able to sue in that country.

The initial presumption is that the action ought to take place where the tort (a wrong) (defamation, in this case) is committed. In other words, the claimant will need to establish sufficient connection with the jurisdiction in which he or she is seeking to bring the action. Second, in the case of defamation, the claimant will need to show that, within that jurisdiction, he or she has a reputation of a sufficient magnitude to uphold.

Now, in terms of our analysis, the two principles in the preceding paragraph come from the Court of Appeal decision in *Chadha v. Dow Jones & Company [1999] EWCA (Civ) 1415*. You will have observed that this case predates the Don King case by some five years. Also, the case did not concern the Internet but magazines printed in the USA and shipped to other countries in the world. Of 294,346 copies of the offending magazines published in the USA, only 1,250 were sent to the UK. So, while the case may be relevant in helping to determine what the position should be vis-à-vis the Internet it can, as lawyers might say, 'be distinguished' from the present case on the facts.

There was another important decision of the House of Lords cited in the *Don King* case – that of *Berezovsky v. Michaels & Others [2000] 1 WLR 1004*. Once again, though, it is not directly relevant to our example because, like *Chadha,* it dealt with a magazine published in the USA and distributed overseas, not alleged libel on the Internet.

The case I would like you to consider in this illustration that is of direct relevance is *Gutnick v. Dow Jones [2002] HCA 56*. This case was a decision of the High Court of Australia and deals directly with the issue of Internet libel. Please look at the *Don King* case and you will see that the decision and reasoning in the Australian decision was influential in helping the Court of Appeal come to its decision. The High Court in Australia rejected an argument that there should be a separate body of law relating to Internet libel as opposed to 'ordinary' libel. My advice is to look closely at the language adopted by the Court of Appeal as a measure of the influence the decision had on members of the court. Here are some examples.

Para. 28

'...the court made certain observations about Internet publication which, with respect, we think we may usefully bear in mind.'

This is a form of words used by judges to indicate that the reasoning impresses them, although they are not 'bound' or obliged to follow the reasoning because the decision was not delivered by a higher court in this jurisdiction.

The Court of Appeal then quotes three paragraphs from the Australian decision. Each makes important points:

39. It was suggested that the World Wide Web was different from radio and television because the radio or television broadcaster could decide how far the signal was to be broadcast. It must be recognised, however, that satellite broadcasting now permits very wide dissemination of radio and television and it may, therefore, be doubted that it is right to say that the World Wide Web has a uniquely broad reach. It is no more or less ubiquitous (present everywhere) than some television services. In the end, pointing to the breadth or depth of reach of particular forms of communication may tend to obscure one basic fact. However broad may be the reach of any particular means of communication, those who post information on the World Wide Web do so knowing that the information they make available is available to all and sundry without geographic restriction.

181. A publisher, particularly one carrying on the business of publishing, does not act to put matter on the Internet in order for it to reach a small target. It is its ubiquity which is one of the main attractions to users of it. And any person who gains access to the Internet does so by taking an initiative to gain access to it in a manner analogous to the purchase or other acquisition of a newspaper, in order to read it.

192. ... Comparisons can, as I have already exemplified, readily be made. If a publisher publishes in a multiplicity of jurisdictions it should understand, and must accept, that it runs the risk of liability in those jurisdictions in which the publication is not lawful and inflicts damage.

To conclude this example, the message that I hope you picked up on is that you must look carefully at recent case law and do not ignore references to overseas court decisions as they can still be relevant. You will of course have to exercise judgement as to whether or not those decisions are significant and that judgement will be assisted by words suggesting that there has been a reliance on, or at least a strong endorsement of, the reasoning employed by courts in this jurisdiction. (I will say more about the substantive issues connected with Internet libel in Part Two.)

The second example relates to overseas judgments that the House of Lords did not find persuasive and therefore rejected. We have already referred in passing to the defence of qualified privilege pleaded by newspapers when they have inadvertently libelled someone in the course of what is claimed to be a public interest article. I will go into the law relating to this in more detail in Part Two, but at this stage, I shall use the leading case of *Reynolds v. Times Newspapers Ltd [1999]* to illustrate how overseas cases are used, particularly by the defendants, *The Sunday Times*. Defence counsel for the newspaper was aware of the fact that cases had been decided in Australia and New Zealand. Robertson and Nicol describe it thus in *Media Law* (4th edn, Penguin, 2002, p. 128):

Some better protection for freedom of speech had been forged by judges in the highest courts of Australia and New Zealand, fashioning a public interest defence out of the common law clay of qualified privilege, permitting it to cling to any occasion on which the media took all reasonable care in publishing information believed to be true about government or political matters.

The cases in question are *Lange v. Australian Broadcasting Corporation [1997] 189 CLR* and *Lange v. Atkinson and Australian Consolidated Press NZ Limited [1999] UKPC 26*. It is also worth noting that, in a wide-ranging speech, Lord Nicholls also examined case law from the USA, Canada,

India and South Africa, although undoubtedly the most relevant cases were the ones from the Antipodes. From reading the decision in *Reynolds,* you will also discover that the *Lange v. Atkinson* case was sent by the New Zealand Court of Appeal to the Privy Council in London. The composition of the board hearing the New Zealand case was exactly the same as that in the House of Lords hearing the *Reynolds* appeal. It is instructive to read the Privy Council's decision, not just for its comments on the New Zealand case but also because it makes reference to the *Reynolds* appeal and for the fact that, eventually, it sent the case back to be determined in New Zealand in light of the House's decision in *Reynolds.*

Please ignore, as far as possible, the details of these cases (these will be discussed in Parts Two and Four). The *Reynolds* case is an excellent example or case study of how the highest court in the land gave careful consideration to relevant case law from Australia and New Zealand. In the event, the House decided that it did not want to follow the lead of the Australian High Court, in particular, and adapt the common law to create a new category of privileged material relating to what the Australian court had called 'political information'. Courts sometimes make the point that what is applicable in one jurisdiction is not necessarily appropriate in another. In other words, the reasoning may be sound but, for example, the political environment within which the media works may be different. Therefore, to go along the same route as the overseas jurisdiction is something the courts are not prepared to countenance.

In the Privy Council, Lord Nicholls of Birkenhead delivered the judgment of the Board. One sentence from the judgment illustrates the relevance of overseas decisions. In para.16 he states:

> *Against this somewhat kaleidoscopic background, one feature of all the judgments, New Zealand, Australian and English, stands out with conspicuous clarity: the recognition that striking a balance between freedom of expression and protection of reputation calls for a value judgment which depends upon local political and social conditions.*

Finally, there may be opportunities for you to cite Privy Council decisions to illustrate the point that English jurisprudence on a particular issue will also apply to the country from which the appeal has emanated. Continuing the qualified privilege theme, examine the Privy Council decision in *Bonnick v. Morris & Others (Jamaica) [2002] UKPC 31.* The *Reynolds* decision is cited with approval and, as a bonus in para. 23 of the judgment, the board gave what is probably one of the best and most succinct definitions of 'responsible journalism' that has appeared since:

Reynolds privilege is concerned to provide a proper degree of protection for responsible journalism when reporting matters of public concern. Responsible journalism is the point at which a fair balance is held between freedom of expression on matters of public concern and the reputations of individuals. Maintenance of this standard is in the public interest and the interests of those whose reputations are involved. It can be regarded as the price journalists pay in return for the privilege. If they are to have the benefit of the privilege journalists must exercise due professional skill and care.

It perhaps will come as no surprise to learn that it was Lord Nicholls sitting in the Privy Council who delivered the above words!

Never underestimate the importance of decisions of the Privy Council and those from overseas jurisdictions, particularly countries with common law antecedents. Make a note on the level of impact you believe that the 'persuasive' authorities have had on the decision in the English court and how influential they may be in deciding future cases.

1.2

categorisation

I suggested earlier that, as an aid to learning and revision, you might wish to consider building up a list of important topics linked to major cases, categorised by 'main' subject area and then further broken down in to 'subcategories'. I will illustrate this by reference to the law on *prior restraint*. I have chosen this topic because it is important thematically and also because there has been recent case law at both House of Lords and Court of Appeal levels.

Prior restraint is a topic that will be considered at the outset of your course. The proposition is a simple one. There are those who, for a number of varying reasons, will endeavour to persuade a court that a newspaper or broadcasting company should be prevented from placing information in the public domain. Reasons given may include:

- the publication will cause the defendant embarrassment
- the publication will cause financial loss, loss of status or loss of job

- the publication is defamatory and the defendant wishes to prevent this unwarranted attack on his or her reputation before any damage is done
- the publication is based on confidential information and that information has been obtained illegally or, to put it another way, the defendant's legal right to privacy or commercial confidentiality has been breached (the classic 'kiss and tell' scenario)
- the defendant's life is at risk if the information is published
- the information about to be published will jeopardise national security or has involved a breach of the Official Secrets Act
- in court proceedings, the defendant might attempt to prevent his or her identity being revealed on the basis that it will lead to the identity of a child being publicised and there are no good reasons for the child in question to come under media scrutiny.

So, a court will be invited to issue an injunction preventing, either temporarily or permanently, the publication in question.

In response, the media will be likely to rely on the concept of free speech or freedom of expression. We are probably all aware of the phrase 'publish and be damned'. The media will argue most strongly that, in a democracy, there is a duty to not curtail the 'right' to free speech. It will be said that, after publication, remedies exist to a claimant if the media do in fact get it wrong, for example, by publishing something that afterwards is proved to be totally untrue.

If this argument is not persuasive enough, the media will usually throw in for good measure an appeal to the 'public interest' – that is, disclosure is in the public interest. It may even be expressed in stronger terms, such as what was said in the leading case of *Cream Holdings Limited & Others v. Banerjee & Others [2004] UKHL 44* (Lord Nicholls, para. 10):

> The principal matter the Echo wishes to publish is 'incontestably' a matter of serious public interest. The essential story was one which, whatever its source, no court could properly suppress.

Perhaps one of the strongest judicial statements in favour of the free speech principle is to be found in the words of Brooke LJ, the Vice-President of the Court of Appeal (Civil Division), in the case of *Greene v. Associated Newspapers Limited [2004] EWCA Civ 1462*. It is worth quoting in full and, if given the opportunity, you ought to consider using this statement in coursework or paraphrasing it for examination purposes. The judge said:

> In this country we have a free press. Our press is free to get things right and it is free to get things wrong. It is free to write after the manner of Milton, and it

is free to write in a manner that would make Milton turn in his grave. Blackstone wrote in 1769 that the liberty of the press is essential in a free state, and this liberty consists in laying no previous restraints on publication. 'Every free man,' he said 'has an undoubted right to lay what sentiments he pleases before the public: to forbid this is to destroy the freedom of the press' (Commentaries, Book 4, pp. 151–2 para. 1). It is this freedom that is under challenge in this appeal.

In addition to finding material supporting the concept of freedom of expression or free speech, you should endeavour to find judicial reasoning as it applies to the concept of the public interest. The critical question to be answered is, 'When is it in the public interest to publish a story?' Although there is virtue in emphasising the most recent judicial pronouncements, you are also well advised to attempt to discover whether or not there are judicial comments that have stood the test of time. Read the judgment of Lord Justice Stephenson in *Lion Laboratories Ltd v. Evans [1984] 2 All ER 417*, p. 423. The following statement encapsulates the very essence of the concept of the 'public interest' and is eminently quotable in assessment situations:

> *There are four considerations. First, 'There is a wide difference between what is interesting to the public and what it is in the public interest to make known' … the public are interested in many private matters which are no real concern of theirs and which the public has no pressing need to know.*
>
> *Second, the media have a private interest of their own in publishing what appeals to the public and may increase circulation or the numbers of their viewers or listeners; and … they are particularly vulnerable to the error of confusing the public interest with their own interest.*
>
> *Third there are cases in which the public interest is best served by an informer giving the confidential information not to the press but to the police or some other responsible body.*
>
> *Fourth, 'there is no confidence as to the disclosure of iniquity' – or, to put it another way, it is in the public interest to disclose wrongdoing, grave misconduct or serious misdeeds.*

Once you have stated the above as a means of indicating to your examiner that you are conscious of what the term stands for, you need to make one further statement. This relates to how a court will respond when the public interest defence is raised. The Court of Appeal in *Lion* (p. 418(c)) put it this way:

> *[The court] ... had to go on to weigh the competing interests of, on the one hand, the public interest in preserving the rights of organisations and of individuals to maintain the secrecy of confidential information against, on the other, the interest of the public to be informed of matters which were of real public concern.*

You might wish to suggest that the court would look favourably on the right to publish once a strong case for a public interest defence has been made. To support your assertion, you could quote Griffiths LJ in the *Lion* case (p. 435(e)) to the effect that:

> *When the press raise the defence of public interest, the court must appraise it critically, but, if convinced that a strong case has been made out, the press should be free to publish, leaving the plaintiff to his remedy in damages.*

Lion Laboratories made a device called the Intoximeter that was used by police forces in the UK for breath testing in suspected drink-driving cases. Two ex-employees delivered company documents to the *Daily Express* newspaper that purported to show there were faults inherent in the breath testing machines that could lead to motorists being wrongly convicted of a serious criminal offence. Undoubtedly the documents were regarded by the company as confidential and it was accepted that the two ex-employees had no right to the documents and had removed them from the company in breach of their contract. The company sought, and initially was granted, an injunction preventing the newspaper from publishing details from the confidential documents.

The Court of Appeal allowed the newspaper's appeal and lifted the injunction. The Court said that the defendants had made a 'powerful case' for publication in the public interest and that it was 'unquestionably in the public interest that information which showed that such an instrument was not reliable should be made public.'

So, you simply ask yourself, 'Are the sentiments expressed over two decades ago still pertinent today?' Of course, this is a point that you will need to research as new cases may have appeared since this book was published. However, you may care to make one point from recent case law. Some judges are asking the question, 'Is the matter under consideration one of public *concern*' and, if they answer the question positively, then accept that the media is under a duty to publish. One example is the case of *Grobbelaar v. News Group Newspapers [2001] EWCA Civ 33*, which involved *The Sun* newspaper printing allegations that the former Liverpool and Southampton goalkeeper, Bruce Grobbelaar, had accepted bribes from representatives of a Far Eastern betting syndicate in order to 'throw' matches. Parker LJ, (para 201) commenting on the seriousness of the allegations said:

> *In my view, allegations of corruption against a well-known professional footballer are plainly a matter of public concern ... without the incentive of being in a position to publish an exclusive story on a sensational subject a newspaper will inevitably be less enthusiastic about committing its time and resources to investigating the story.*

In *Armstrong v. Times Newspapers & Others [2004] EWHC 2928 (QB)*, Eady J used the same terminology when considering whether or not *The Sunday Times* was under a duty to publish the story regarding the allegation that Lance Armstrong, the cycling star, had taken performance-enhancing drugs: *'Secondly, the subject matter is, I am prepared to assume, one of public concern.'* (para 83)

Each of the cases mentioned above concerned the defence of qualified privilege being pleaded by the newspapers and not an issue of prior restraint. The question for you to ponder is, 'Should it make a difference whether one is considering public interest or public concern in the context of prior restraint or qualified privilege?'

In each case, the newspaper in question believes that the information should be in the public domain because of the seriousness of the subject matter. However, an analysis of the concept of 'public interest', in the context of prior restraint when the claimant is seeking an injunction to prevent alleged defamatory material being published, finds one of the latest cases reaffirming the principles laid down over a century ago. In *Bonnard v. Perryman [1891] 2 Ch 269*, (at p. 284) Lord Chief Justice Coleridge stated his belief that freedom of the press was synonymous with the public interest:

> *The right of free speech is one which it is for the public interest that individuals should possess and indeed that they should exercise without impediment ...*

So, your learning aid and revision note might look something like this:

Course Segment: Introduction

Topic title: Law on prior restraint

Key themes

- Free speech/expression
- Public interest/public concern
- Injunctions

Statutes

- Human Rights Act 1998
- Defamation Act 1996

Case Law

- *Cream Holdings [2004] HL* *****
- *Re. S(FC) (a child) [2004] HL* *****
- *Greene v. Associated Press [2004] CA* *****
- *Bonnard v. Perryman [1891]* *****
- *Lion Laboratories v. Evans [1984] CA* *****

European Jusiprudence
Observer & Guardian v. UK (1992) ****
European Convention on Human Rights, Article 10, Freedom of expression

I have not made the list all-embracing, in the sense that I have included a long list of cases that might in some small way be relevant to the issue – that is not the purpose of the exercise. Having taken into account the emphasis being placed on the topic by your tutor, you must identify the key pieces of information that it is absolutely imperative to mention in your coursework or examinations. This is assuming, of course, that you wish to progress and achieve something higher than a borderline pass!

You may wish to continue in the same vein for each topic, identifying key points that you wish to make, together with reasons. It could look something like this:

Topic: Prior restraint points to emphasise

- Importance of freedom of speech in a democracy.
- Principles of European Convention on Human Rights, integrated into UK law from 2 October 2000.
- S.12 Human Rights Act makes special provision regarding freedom of expression.

- Pay special attention to s.12(3) of the HRA. Purpose to 'buttress the protection afforded to freedom of speech at the interlocutory stage.' What are the chances of success if the case comes to trial? Legal meaning of the word 'likely' in s.12(3). See *Cream Holdings*, s.12(3), a 'statutory threshold' in cases of prior restraint.
- Issue of prior restraint usually encompasses discussion on breach of confidentiality and/or privacy.
- News becomes stale very quickly. If injunctions are readily granted to prevent the press from publishing, then form of censorship being imposed. Contrary to the assumptions underpinning the Convention.
- Other rights have to be balanced, particularly rights to reputation. Lord Nicholls in *Reynolds* refers to freedom of expression and right to reputation as 'fundamental rights.'
- Public interest concept must be articulated. See four elements identified in *Lion* case.
- Recent case law very supportive of the right to publish. HL in *Cream*.
- Note distinction between cases involving breach of confidentiality and those involving alleged defamatory material. Right to sue not lost in latter case, freedom to publish upheld. See *Greene v. Associated Press [2004]*.

1.3	
themes	

As you read this part of the book, it will probably become increasingly apparent that certain themes can be identified that permeate a number of elements of your media law course. Let us look at two of them next.

Privacy and freedom of expression

The concept of the *public interest* is one that has been referred to earlier. Another, which has had a far greater impact on media law, is the Human Rights Act 1998, together with the European Convention on Human

Rights. If you consider the first schedule to the Human Rights Act, you will soon discover the extent to which the various articles of the Convention can impact media law. There are clearly two articles that are pivotal for the media and hold the potential for an increasing level of judicial intervention. Judges will need to resolve what appears to be a clash between the right of an individual to protect his or her private life (Article 8) and the right of the media to freely express views and opinions (Article 10). This is an issue that you must bear in mind when dealing with the 'privacy' unit of your course.

Before you try to come to grips with the legal issues that have arisen since the Act came into force in 2000, it will be invaluable to consider the purpose underpinning the legislation. After all, the European Convention dates back to the 1950s, so how come we are so late in incorporating its provisions into our law, despite the fact that Britain was the first country to endorse the Convention in 1953?

A useful, albeit relatively simplistic, source to help answer this question is the introduction to the legislation produced by the government and available on the Department for Constitutional Affairs website (www.dca.gov.uk). This tells us that 'Fifty years ago Britain helped to enshrine our basic liberties into the European Convention on Human Rights.' No longer is there a need to go to Strasbourg to enforce those rights as the introduction of the Human Rights Act 'means that we can safeguard our rights here in the UK. And we can be clearer about the basic values and standards we share.' So said the then Home Secretary Jack Straw and the Lord Chancellor Lord Irvine of Lairg. Spend a few more minutes reading the introduction and you will discover that the document refers to 'fundamental rights and freedoms in the European Convention on Human Rights.' This reflects the language that we constantly hear judges using when dealing with human rights matters. For example, the comment of Lord Nicholls in *Reynolds* (at p. 8):

> My starting point is freedom of expression. The high importance of
> freedom to impart and receive information and ideas has been
> stated so often and so eloquently that this point calls for no elaboration ...
> Freedom of expression will shortly be buttressed by statutory requirements.
> Under section 12 of the Human Rights Act ... the court is required, in
> relevant cases, to have particular regard to the importance of the right to
> freedom of expression. The common law is to be developed and applied in a
> manner consistent with Article 10 of the ... Convention and the court must
> take into account relevant decisions of the European Court of Human Rights.

To be justified, any curtailment of freedom of expression must be convincingly established by a compelling countervailing consideration, and the means employed must be proportionate to the end sought to be achieved.

In case you are worried about over-reliance on statements by Lord Nicholls, you may care to quote Lord Steyn in the same case. In speaking of a 'new legal landscape' and the 'constitutional dimension of freedom of expression [being] reinforced', he stated (at p. 14):

The starting point is now the right of freedom of expression, a right based on a constitutional or higher legal order foundation. Exceptions to freedom of expression must be justified as being necessary in a democracy.

It is also worth making the point that, as the Human Rights Bill was being discussed in Parliament, concern was expressed on behalf of the media that freedom of expression was to be given no greater weighting than any other article in the Convention. Parliament's response was to insert section 12 into the Act with the intention that it should serve to remind judges of the overriding importance of freedom of expression, particularly when action was to be taken against media interests! Although the wording doesn't necessarily make this clear, the alleged intention underpinning the section has penetrated judicial thinking, as we clearly saw from the decision in *Cream Holdings [2004]*.

Section 12, Freedom of expression, is cast in the following terms:

(1) This section applies if a court is considering whether to grant any relief which, if granted, might affect the exercise of the Convention right to freedom of expression.

(2) Not relevant in this context.

(3) No such relief is to be granted so as to restrain publication before trial unless the court is satisfied that the applicant is likely to establish that publication should not be allowed.

(4) The court must have particular regard to the importance of the Convention right to freedom of expression and, where the proceedings relate to material which the respondent claims, or which appears to the court, to be journalistic, literary or artistic material (or to conduct connected to such material) to

(a) The extent to which

    (i) the material has, or is about to, *become available to the public; or*

    (ii) it is, *or* would be, *in the public interest for the material to be published;*

(b) any *relevant privacy code.*

(5) Not relevant in this context.

You will see that I have emphasised certain words that are likely to need judicial consideration. Please consider the words of section 12(4), which places an obligation on a court to have not just *regard* but *particular* regard to the right of free expression. A major concern of the media at the time of the Bill's passage through Parliament was to ensure that their activities would not be curtailed as a result of individuals – usually celebrities – invoking Article 8. The concern was that the courts would respond by taking the law beyond the ambit of 'public authority' intrusion into private lives. You should, though, query the inclusion of subsection 4(b), which directs the court to consider the terms of any privacy code.

The relevant code for the newspaper industry is the Press Complaints Commission's Code of Practice and that for broadcasters being the Broadcasting Code of 2005. However, these codes provide no *remedies* and, therefore, the court must simply consider whether or not, in a privacy or confidentiality action, the media representatives have adhered to their own code of practice. If they haven't, to use a football analogy, the media will be one down with the match having only just kicked off!

In your desire to emphasise section 12, please do not forget to make passing reference to section 3, interpretation of legislation:

(1) So far as it is possible to do so, *primary legislation and subordinate legislation* must *be read and given effect in a way which is compatible with the Convention rights.*

This is a powerful instruction to judges that they must adopt a construction that supports the media's right to free speech in accordance with Article 10. As Lord Slynn said in *Regina v. Lambert [2001] UKHL 37,* (para 6) albeit when dealing with a drugs appeal:

It is clear that the 1998 Act must be given its full import and that long and well entrenched ideas may have to be put aside, sacred cows culled.

> You should always consider when answering any question whether or not and to what extent you need to refer to the Human Rights Act. This may be in general terms, such as reference to the aims and objectives of the legislation, or it may be to specific sections that have attracted judicial attention, in the English courts or the European Court of Human Rights.

European jurisprudence

Another theme that runs through a significant number of topics within a media law syllabus is the importance of emphasising, where appropriate, the increasing importance of European jurisprudence on this jurisdiction. One point that should be made at the outset in answers where you do mention it is to refer the examiner to section 2 of the Human Rights Act, Interpretation of Convention rights. It states that a court or tribunal involved in determining a question that has arisen in connection with a Convention right must *take into account* any:

> judgment, decision, declaration or advisory opinion of the European Court of Human Rights ... [providing] it is relevant to the proceedings in which that question has arisen.

However, to state this will invariably not be enough. You will need to expand on your reference by making the point that section 2 does not force a court to follow or apply the European Court's reasoning. Rather, a court in this jurisdiction has to 'take it into account' and only then when it is relevant to the proceedings in question. So, just because the European Court decided in a particular way does not mean that the English courts will do the same.

A relatively recent example will serve to illustrate the point, although the question decided by the European Court of Human Rights has still to be tested in this jurisdiction. The example relates to the protection of privacy rights. This country does not have a discrete tort of privacy. For years, if individuals wished to protect their 'privacy', they would have to 'fit' their circumstances into the law of confidentiality. However, even a cursory look at the law relating to confidentiality shows that, in the main, the protection offered by the law related to 'information' rather than the 'broader' concept of privacy. To succeed in this, the plaintiff would have had to conform to the principles and circumstances enunciated by the Court of Appeal in the case of *Saltman Engineering*

Co. Ltd v. Campbell Engineering Co. Ltd (1948) [1963] 3 All ER 413. They were summarised by Megarry J in *Coco v. A.N. Clark (Engineers) Ltd [1969] RPC 41(at p. 4)* in the following terms:

> In my judgment, three elements are normally required if, apart from contract, a case of breach of confidence is to succeed. First, the information itself, in the words of Lord Greene MR in the Saltman case must 'have the necessary quality of confidence about it.' Secondly, that information must have been imparted in circumstances importing an obligation of confidence. Thirdly, there must be an unauthorised use of that information to the detriment of the party communicating it.

So, in a case like *Stephens v. Avery [1988] 2 All ER 477*, it is easy to see from the facts of the case why the law on confidentiality was entirely appropriate. The plaintiff had imparted personal information to her close friend on the express basis that what she had been told should remain secret. In other words, it was a 'confidential communication'. The information was by way of a confession that she had been the lesbian lover of a woman who had subsequently been killed by her husband who was convicted of her manslaughter. The trial attracted a lot of press publicity and the information relating to the deceased woman's affair was mentioned in court, but the plaintiff was not named at the trial. The recipient of the information, Mrs Avery, had passed it on to the then Editor of the *Mail on Sunday*. The Editor was the second defendant and the newspaper group the third defendant when Mrs Stephens sought damages for breach of confidence.

The court gave Mrs Stephens permission to go ahead with her action against the defendants.

What of those, particularly celebrities, who desired less press intrusion into their lives. How could they prevent – or should they even be legally allowed to prevent – media intrusion in their lives when a privacy law did not exist in this country? In a celebrated case in 1977, Tom Jones and two other pop singers brought an action aimed at preventing their former public relations and press officer from revealing details of their private lives in a series of articles in the *Daily Mirror*. They claimed that the articles were written in breach of confidence, based as they were on information gleaned in the course of his employment.

In a notable judgment, Lord Denning refused to grant an injunction preventing the publication of the 'confidential information' on the basis that those who sought publicity to their advantage could not complain if publicity was also given to matters that revealed them in a less favourable light.

The issue faced by the European Court of Human Rights in 2004 was different and by no stretch of the imagination could it be brought within the ambit of the law on confidentiality. It demonstrated the importance of Article 8 of the Convention. The question posed is a simple one: 'To what degree, if any, is a celebrity entitled to protect his or her private life from media scrutiny?' Think about the situations that may arise because they are likely to be ones that you will have to analyse as part of an examination question. Let us use the word 'celebrity' in the *Oxford Dictionary* sense of 'well-known person'. It would therefore include politicians, royalty, sports stars, film stars, media people and those with dubious reputations to protect.

The European Court of Human Rights case in 2004 that we are taking as an example is *Von Hannover v. Germany [2004]*. Princess Caroline of Monaco, the daughter of Prince Ranier, and his film actress wife, Grace Kelly (Princess Grace), has campaigned long and hard to protect her privacy from the lenses of the paparazzi. She is married to Prince Ernst August Von Hannover, her third husband. A number of German magazines over a number of years carried photographs of Princess Caroline doing everyday things – described in the *International Herald Tribune* in October 2004 as, 'benign enough to fill a staid family scrapbook.' Some examples (and these are worth noting when considering the decision) are:

- four photographs in *Bunte* magazine in March 1997 showing her leaving her house in Paris, with the caption, 'Out and about with Princess Caroline in Paris?'
- seven photographs showing Princess Caroline on the front page of *Bunte* with Prince Ernst and, on the inside pages of the magazine, playing tennis with him or both of them putting their bicycles down
- a number of photographs, again in *Bunte* magazine, showing her doing her shopping, alone on her bicycle and with her young son who is carrying a bunch of flowers
- photographs showing her on a skiing holiday.

No doubt you can visualise the types of photographs published in this and other German celebrity magazines. She claimed that German laws did not provide her with enough protection against paparazzi intrusion when she was simply going about her private business. She made no complaint about photographs of her being taken if she were attending a public or media event, such as a film gala, or working in a representative capacity on behalf of her husband or the Monaco Royal Family. In other words, when she was acting in an 'official' capacity. She quite simply felt that her Article 8 rights were being breached as a result of photographic intrusion into her family and personal life. It is also worth pointing out that some of the photographs had been taken secretly and were not of the highest quality – the 'long lens' shots that we are all so familiar with from our tabloid newspapers. She had made several applications to the German courts for protection, but had failed on each occasion, hence she took the case to Strasbourg.

The European Court of Human Rights concluded that her Article 8 rights had been breached. Your task as a student is to discover the reasons for the decision and to consider whether or not the English courts are likely to adopt the decision and for it to become part of English law at some future stage.

When reading a case report, it is helpful if you can simply make a list of key points in bullet form that you can expand on at a later stage. So with the Caroline decision, your key points might look something like the following list.

- Was German law compatible with Article 8?
- Did German law strike the correct balance between freedom of expression and respect for private and family life?
- ECHR had 'no doubt' that photographing Caroline in her 'daily life' fell within the scope of her private life. Article 8 therefore applicable.
- Court noted that photographs of the type published in this case were often taken in a climate of 'continual harassment leaving a strong sense of intrusion into private life or even feeling of persecution.'
- Court considered the decisive factor in balancing Articles 8 and 10 'should lie in the contribution that the photographs and articles made to a debate of "general interest".'
- The photographs at the heart of this case had been taken without Caroline's consent or knowledge and, in some instances, in secret.
- The photographs made no contribution to a debate of public interest since they related 'exclusively to details of her private life.'
- Court recognised that the public had a right to information ... but not in this instance. Public had no 'legitimate interest' in knowing her whereabouts or how she behaved generally in her private life. This covered places that were not necessarily 'secluded and may have been well known to the public.'
- The Court believed that there had to be *effective* protection for the applicant's private life.
- What reasons did Court give for protecting private life? It reiterated the 'fundamental' importance of protection as a means of helping to develop every human being's personality. Even well-known people had to have a 'legitimate expectation that his or her private life would be protected.'
- Court therefore concluded that the German courts had not struck a fair balance between the competing interests and held that there had been a violation of Article 8.

The list would continue by including points on the consequences of the decision if it was applied to the UK.

- As the Court emphasised the importance of the publications contributing to 'a debate of general interest', it would appear that 'celebrity' photographs must adhere to a 'public interest' test in order for the publisher not to be found in breach of an applicant's Article 8 rights. This would also apply to someone who neither holds public office nor is engaged in official duties.
- If this is the case, then press freedom as we know it, particularly on a Sunday morning, but not excluding the daily tabloids and magazines, may be seriously curtailed. Permission will have to be sought from the subject or a fee paid. The issue of *image rights* begins to merge into privacy issues.
- Questions will also be raised about the relevance of the Press Complaints Commission's (PCC) Code of Practice, to which all journalists are in theory supposed to adhere.
- Celebrities will be in a strong position if the PCC code is breached and the publication does not comply with the 'public interest' or 'debate of general interest' test.

Do consider the impact of decisions of the European Court of Human Rights. They could, in fact, be the harbinger of a legal issue yet to be resolved in the UK and therefore provide potential examination fodder, as with the Caroline case. When dealing with privacy issues, do not forget to make reference to the PCC's Code of Practice as you will recall that, under section 12(4) of the Human Rights Act, the English courts are meant to have 'particular regard' to the privacy provisions of the PCC's Code of Practice when considering matters relating to freedom of expression.

In conclusion, you might care to consider some of the adjudications made by the PCC in matters where the applicant has claimed that the privacy clause has been breached.

Clause 3 of the code relates to privacy and states:

(i) *Everyone is entitled to respect for his or her private and family life, home, health and correspondence, including digital communications. Editors will be expected to justify intrusions into any individual's private life without consent.*

(ii) *It is unacceptable to photograph individuals in private places without their consent.*

Note that 'private places' are public or private property where there is a reasonable expectation of privacy. The *Caroline* decision, if implemented in England and Wales, will undoubtedly lead to this clause being amended.

The code can ·be downloaded from the PCC's website (at www. pcc.org.uk). Having accessed the website, I would urge you to spend a few minutes trawling through past adjudications for the following reasons.

- The code deals with many aspects of media practice, so it is helpful for you to know how the profession believes it should operate.
- The code has often been heralded as providing 'quasi-judicial' remedies. It does nothing of the sort. Industry insiders sit in judgment on their colleagues. A complaint may be upheld – that is, even the insiders believe the newspaper has gone too far but it does nothing to provide compensation or anything equivalent or vaguely reminiscent of a judicial remedy. Its decisions will often be reported, but not in any high-profile way or in a prominent position in a newspaper.
- From the privacy viewpoint, it will help identify situations in which individuals, whether celebrities or not, have felt aggrieved at the actions of the press and brought a complaint. Here are three examples.

  - The Commission ruled on 29 August 2004 on a complaint by **Kimberly Fortier** that, following the revelations that she had pursued an affair with the then Home Secretary, she was photographed in Los Angeles while walking with her son. Her lawyers complained to newspaper editors that to publish would breach the harassment and privacy provisions of the code as she had made it clear to the photographer that she did not wish to be photographed.

    - In her complaint to the Commission, she also stated that she was not a public figure and the *Sunday Mirror,* against which the complaint was lodged, argued that, as a result of the affair, she had become a public figure and was a legitimate target.
    - The Commission rejected both complaints. In respect of the privacy clause, it said that she had been photographed in a public place and this would not normally be seen as a breach of the code. In addition, because of the relationship with the then Home Secretary, which had not been denied, the photograph and story made a contribution to general debate on a matter of public interest.

  - In October 2002, Julie Goodyear, who had for many years played the part of Bet Lynch, the barmaid at the Rovers Return in *Coronation Street,* complained about long-lens photographs of her taken while she was sitting in her garden. The photographs were published in *The People* newspaper. The Commission upheld her complaint, based on the reasonable expectation of privacy when in her own back garden.
  - In September 2000, Anna Ford, a BBC newsreader, complained about photographs published in the *Daily Mail* and *OK* magazine. They showed her with a male companion while on holiday in Majorca on a beach wearing

swimwear. She claimed that she understood the beach on which they were situated was private and not public and as such had a reasonable expectation of privacy (see also the judicial review case *Anna Ford v. Press Complaints Commission [2001] EWHC Admin 683*).

- The complaint was rejected on the basis that 'a publicly accessible Majorcan beach was not a place where the complainants could have had a reasonable expectation of privacy.

- You may care to ponder whether in the first and third examples, the applicant's rights under Article 8 of the Convention might have been breached given the Court's decision in the *Caroline* case.

1.4
thinking like a journalist

If you are in training to become a journalist, you will, of necessity, have to adopt a more 'practical' approach to media law. The law is often viewed as a 'background' subject, albeit an increasingly important one. While you will be made aware of key themes, such as the public interest and freedom of expression, the emphasis in the course is likely to be on 'trade-craft' issues.

The major areas for consideration in this context will be defamation, reporting restrictions and court reporting in general, contempt of court and how journalists protect their sources. These topics, particularly defamation, will also feature in a 'conventional' media law course, but, if you are a degree student, you may well spend less time on them than trainee journalists.

The expectations of tutors will also be somewhat different. There will be a desire for you to demonstrate that you are aware of the legal principles within which you are expected to operate in practice. This will include knowledge of important statutes, together with major common law principles. You will need to show a detailed appreciation of legislation, such as the Contempt of Court Act 1981 and the Children and Young Person's Act 1933. There will also be an expectation that you will be familiar with more recent legislation with important messages for journalists. I am thinking of statutes such as the Sexual Offences Act 2002, the Youth Justice and Criminal Evidence Act 1999, the Criminal Justice Act 2003 (bad character provisions) and the Freedom of Information Act 2000 (effective from 1 January 2005).

It is in this context that *MacNae's Essential Law for Journalists* can be both a strength and, like the majority of law books, a weakness. The strength is that it takes a journalist's perspective on the law; the weakness is that the law moves on quickly and the statutory provisions relied on in the book may have been superseded.

As a trainee journalist, you should therefore prioritise your learning. Become as familiar as possible with the legal provisions within which you will operate. You would, for example, not wish to embarrass yourself by using a mobile phone in court or using it to take a photograph of the defendant, however attractive that proposition might seem. There have been examples of this happening and one perpetrator was imprisoned for six months for contempt. Thankfully the isolated incidents have not involved journalists.

Nor would you wish to report more than the law allows you to when covering committal proceedings or defaming someone by failing to carry out adequate research before filing your story. Two recent examples of the latter will serve to illustrate the point. The first involves what, at the time, was the oldest horse in Britain. In January 2004, reports appeared in a number of newspapers alleging that a 51-year-old horse named Badger had been neglected to a degree amounting to gross cruelty by his carers – a vet and his qualified riding instructor wife. The horse had been kept at the livery yard owned by the couple and received veterinary care from the husband. The article also alleged that the horse was in a 'shocking and disgusting state and was on the brink of starvation' when transferred into the care of the Veteran Horse Society in October 2003.

The newspapers concerned, including the *Daily Mirror* and *Daily Mail,* were forced into an embarrassing climbdown after being sued for defamation by the couple. The statement agreed by the lawyers acting for the couple and the newspapers acknowledged that the allegations were untrue and went on to state that the couple 'had treated Badger as their own, paying for most of his care and keep, which his owner could not afford. The care provided was competent and appropriate, meaning Badger's condition was remarkably good for his great age.' Damages and costs were paid to the couple.

The obvious question is how could the reporter have got the story so wrong? Remember, this is an era when the courts (per *Reynolds*) look to establish whether or not there is evidence of 'responsible journalism' in defamation cases where qualified privilege could be pleaded as a defence.

The second example is even more startling. The Saudi Arabian Ambassador to the UK had been accused by the magazine *Paris Match* of being directly responsible for the 9/11 atrocity in the USA. The article included a statement that Prince Turki Al-Faisal had given $200 million to Osama Bin Laden in return for his agreeing not to attack Saudi Arabia but gave him carte blanche to cause destruction elsewhere in the world.

The publishers apologised, accepted that there was no truth in any of the allegations and withdrew them unreservedly. In addition, a substantial but undisclosed amount in damages was paid to Prince Al-Faisal.

Once again, the question must be asked as to how the magazine could publish a story that, on the face of it, contained little if anything that resembled the truth. The price of failure can be huge!

You should also keep a weather eye out for new legislative provisions that may be introduced during your period of study. This is for two reasons. The first obviously is because you may be asked in your assessment about the impact of a new provision on existing law. The second is that you will be more likely to convince at interview for that all important job you've applied for if you can show that you are aware of the most recent legislative provisions and their impacts on the life of a working journalist. A good example is the implementation of section 93 of the Courts Act 2003 on 18 October 2004. Section 93 gives a court the power to make what are called third party costs orders where there has been *serious misconduct* that results in a trial being delayed or aborted. The most obvious way this can occur is when the media, due to prejudicial reporting prior to or during a trial, finds itself in contempt of court.

- *Construct your learning plan in the following way:*
- *identify key pieces of legislation, particularly those that will have practical implications for you as a journalist*
- *identify any pending legislative provision that may become law during your course, such as the bad character provisions in the Criminal Justice Act 2003*
- *identify the leading cases that have everyday practical implications, such as* Reynolds, *and other important cases that establish a principle, such as* Cream Holdings, *or from a European perspective, the Princess* Caroline *case*
- *note that the questions set in your examinations will require you to look at the law from a journalistic perspective rather than from a 'black letter' lawyer's perspective, but you still must make correct statements of legal principle.*

A clear example is the abandoning of the trial at Hull Crown Court in 2001 of the footballers Jonathan Woodgate and Lee Bowyer on charges of causing an affray and grievous bodily harm with intent. The trial lasted for ten weeks and the jury, which had retired for the weekend, was still considering its decision when the *Sunday Mirror* published a two-page spread that consisted of an interview with the father of the young student allegedly attacked by the footballers. In the article, the father had raised issues about racial violence and stated that he wished he had left Britain so that his son would not have been exposed to racial abuse. The legal issue was that the judge had specifically ruled that the case did not have a racial element. The article, therefore, was likely to confuse members of the jury who saw it and raise the question of whether or not the jury could carry out its job of deciding the matter based purely on the evidence it had heard in court.

In the event, the trial was abandoned, at a cost to the taxpayer of over £1 million. The retrial, at which Woodgate was found guilty of affray and Bowyer acquitted on all charges, was reputed to have cost £1.1 million.

The Attorney General brought contempt proceedings against the *Sunday Mirror,* to which it pleaded guilty and a fine of £75,000 was imposed. The newspaper argued that it had never intended to create a substantial risk that the proceedings would be seriously impeded or prejudiced. However, it failed to explain how the piece came to be published despite assurances to the young man's father that the article would not be published until *after* the trial had been concluded. The *Sunday Mirror* accepted that it had been wrong to run the story and assured the court that it had strengthened its procedures for checking stories.

If these events had been played out after 18 October 2004, the *Sunday Mirror* might well have found itself having to pick up some or all of the costs of the abandoned trial and the retrial. There are several concerns for journalists arising from this legislation and that is why attention needs to be paid to this section. First, the trial judge will deal with the matter of 'serious misconduct', which is not defined in the Act. In the case of the footballers, the trial had lasted ten weeks prior to the article appearing and it is safe to assume that the judge was not best pleased when he was made aware of it. If the same thing happened today, the judge could impose a costs order against the newspaper without having to refer the matter to the Attorney General for possible contempt proceedings. At the moment, it is unknown how the amount of the order would be determined. From the media's perspective, if the courts impose high costs, then this could be seen as having a 'chilling' effect on freedom of expression. The media will have to think carefully about how it reports prior to and during trials.

The sort of situation that can easily arise is detailed below:

A serious fraud trial was due to commence in a Crown Court in the south of England but an article appeared in the local daily newspaper which was 'unfair, inaccurate and prejudicial.' The errors were repeated the following day with an inflammatory headline and photographs of the defendants. The judge was forced to stop the trial from proceeding and discharge the jury because the defendants risked not receiving a fair trial. The jurors could potentially have seen the headline, read the articles and formed a view that was based on 'factually wrong' reporting rather than on evidence put before them. The judge said 'I must consider the extent to which the publicity has created a risk of prejudice in this trial so grave that no direction by me [to the jury], however careful, could reasonably be expected to remove it.' The trial was rescheduled six months later to another location where the jurors were unlikely to have heard about the case. (Government News Network, September 2004)

For an actual example of where prejudicial reporting would now in all probability attract a costs order, see the case *In the Matter of an application by Her Majesty's Attorney General for Northern Ireland [2003] NIQB 73.*

The Attorney General brought contempt proceedings against Belfast Telegraph Newspapers Ltd relating to a number of articles about one Sean Toner shortly before his trial on drugs charges. The accused was due to stand trial on 22 September 2002. The *Sunday Life* newspaper ran three articles – on 3 March 2002, 28 July 2002 and 15 September 2002 – in which numerous aspects of Sean Toner's criminal career were detailed. The final article, one week before he was due to stand trial, was headed 'Fugitive Dealer Busted'. In it, he was described as a drugs dealer and the article went on to give details of his links to a murder and the fact that he fled Ulster after escaping from a drugs squad raid on his home.

The Editor, no doubt aware of the seriousness of the matter, explained that the journalist who was the author of the final article believed the trial 'would not take place for some considerable time.' On what basis he believed that is not explained. A quick phone call to the Crown Court would have given him all the information he needed to make an informed decision on whether or not the article would be contemptuous if published at that time. In expressing his regret to the court, he lamely added that, 'The staff of the newspaper had undergone training on the law of contempt.'

The court imposed fines for contempt totalling £5,000. Under the Courts Act 2003, however, if the trial judge had concluded that there had been serious misconduct and that had been the cause of the trial being delayed, then a third party costs order would be deemed appropriate.

1.5

conclusion

In this part of the book, I have outlined some of the key themes that will surface on a media law course. I have also urged you to adopt learning practices consistent with the type of programme that you are undertaking. I believe that it is important for you to consider primary sources so I have not referred to articles in academic or professional journals.

As to tutors' expectations, I have made a number of general assumptions, but only by questioning your tutor will you discover exactly what you are expected to deliver.

Throughout your course, your answers to questions should show that you are aware of the major pieces of legislation and case law, English and European, relevant to this subject. In relation to case law, you do not need to spend too long detailing the facts because it is unlikely that you will be given a problem to assess that exactly parallels the facts of an actual case.

The critical point when learning is to always ask, 'Why has the court decided in this way?' and 'What are the major reasons for the decision?' Tutors will expect you to not only simply describe the law but also *justify* it and show its *applicability* to any given set of facts.

Next, I will examine the elements of the curriculum with which you are likely to have to get to grips with if you wish to gain high marks in your assessment.

part two
curriculum in a nutshell

- Introduction
- An indicative syllabus
- Introductory themes
- Defamation
- Reporting restrictions
- Contempt of court
- Protection of sources
- Privacy and breach of confidentiality
- Elements of intellectual property law

2.1	
introduction	

In this part of the book the focus is on curriculum content. The aim is to identify the essential core elements of the curriculum and highlight the range of content that you will need to come to terms with in order to do yourself justice in the assessment process.

2.2	
an indicative syllabus	

Core Areas
- Introduction
- Defamation
- Reporting restrictions
- Contempt of court
- Protection of sources
- Privacy and breach of confidentiality
- Elements of intellectual property law

Learning outcomes

By the end of Part Two you should be able to:

- Identify the major legal principles relating to the key syllabus areas.
- Appreciate the legal context within which journalists are presumed to operate.
- Recognise the fundamental importance of Articles 6, 8 and 10 of the European Convention on Human Rights to the applications of media law.
- Accept that a good assessment mark will result mainly from a strong analytical approach based upon legal knowledge gained from primary sources and not from a purely 'descriptive' approach to examination answers.

- Understand that the law is never 'static'. Always be on the look-out for the latest cases.
- Understand the role of claimants and defendants in media law actions.

Let me at the outset offer up an indicative syllabus for media law. It is 'indicative' because there are lots of variations but I hope that what appears below does bear more than a passing resemblance to the syllabus you are following.

The syllabus is usually in three parts. The first part normally takes the form of an introduction to the subject and will invariably challenge you to think about some or all of the following:

- entrenched rights to free speech and freedom of expression recognised in documents such as the Constitution of the USA
- how those rights are protected in court action
- The extent and value of such rights.

This may take the form of a theoretical discussion rather than initially focusing on particular examples or case law. However, at some point the theoretical perspective is likely to be enhanced by reference to specific examples in order to ascertain whether or not there is any synergy between the 'theoretical' and 'practical'.

The tactic behind this approach is to show the student that, while we in the UK don't have a written constitution, we do now have European Convention rights incorporated into our law by means of the Human Rights Act 1998. Your tutor may then raise the question as to whether or not the rights of the people of the USA are somehow more 'fundamental' than the rights of citizens of the UK simply because of the existence of entrenched rights and a written constitution.

Just bear in mind the text of the 1st Amendment to the Constitution of the USA:

Congress shall make no law respecting an establishment of religion, or prohibiting the free exercise thereof; or abridging the freedom of speech, or of the press; or the right of the people peaceably to assemble, and to petition the government for a redress of grievance.

Clearly this wording is aimed at the USA's legislature, preventing it from passing laws that curtail freedom of speech or freedom of the press. Congress may, of course, pass laws relating to free speech and a free press, but the clear statement of intent is that courts cannot adopt a construction of those laws that would limit those two rights. As such, they become *fundamental* rights for each and every citizen of the USA.

The UK's legislation is not so emphatic. You may recall that section 3 of the Human Rights Act 1998 states:

> So far as it is possible to do so, primary legislation and subordinate legislation must be read and given effect in a way which is compatible with the Convention rights.

The use of the words 'so far as it is possible' would suggest that Parliament is not bestowing inalienable rights on British citizens in the same way as the USA's Constitution purports to do for its citizens.

In addition to a consideration of the theoretical issues related to such concepts, you may be invited to consider the phrases 'public interest' and 'freedom of expression', to which we alluded in Part One, from a *practical* point of view. These are placed in the introductory part of the syllabus because they are likely to surface at various times throughout the course, so you need to be aware of them at the outset.

You are then likely to move on to the substantive issues that form the core elements of the programme. The weighting given to each of these topics may well vary depending on their currency. For example, no examination of media law in the academic year 2005–2006 would have been complete without focusing on the law relating to privacy because of crucial decisions from the High Court *(McKennitt v. Ash [2005]* and *HRH The Prince of Wales v. Associated Newspapers Ltd (No. 3) [2006])*.

Although not a betting man by nature, I would be prepared to invest a few hard-earned pounds in stating that the first substantive element of the law to be considered will be that relating to defamation. At this stage, I will simply outline what is likely to be covered and then return to each to put a little flesh on the skeleton. This topic will include consideration of the law relating to libel and slander and the defences available to those who are sued. The major defences are:

- justification
- fair comment
- privilege, with the likely emphasis on qualified privilege simply because that is the defence most utilised by the media.

Note also that tutors will pick topics that have a substantial body of case law and qualified privilege definitely fits this bill. Depending on the time available, your tutor may consider the role of the jury when deliberating the amount of damages to be awarded if the claimant is successful.

The next topic may well be *reporting restrictions*. It is easy to understand why. In this country, we adhere to a principle that our courts should be open to all and justice should be seen to be done. This is directly related to the recognition of free speech and expression and, therefore, the media claims the right to report what goes on in the courts unhindered. For 90 per cent of the time, you should be focusing on the criminal courts, but, now and then, the press needs to be aware of its obligations when dealing with the civil courts, particularly in cases involving children and in family proceedings.

So, the questions you will be faced with include the following.

- What restrictions are there?
- What is the justification for any restriction?
- How might the press challenge any restriction imposed by a court?
- What are the chances of a challenge succeeding?

The press must adhere to the Article 6 right of a defendant to receive a fair trial and, therefore, their reporting must not prejudice that trial. This will then link in neatly to the next important topic.

Contempt of court is a voluminous topic and has multiple strands. You will need to become familiar with the provisions of the Contempt of Court Act (CCA) 1981. The relationship between *common law* and *statutory* contempt will also need to be appreciated. The specific aspects of the law that will feature are:

- the strict liability rule
- when proceedings are *active*
- the meaning of 'substantial risk of prejudice' to proceedings
- postponement orders and how to challenge them (section 4(2) CCA)
- innocent publication
- 'public affairs' defence
- limitations on reporting connected with juries
- misuse of tape recorders in court
- protection of sources, although this is likely to feature as a topic in its own right (section 10 of the CCA)
- when section 11 orders are appropriate (CCA).

So, the major focus will be on the provisions of the legislation. However, I suspect that you will be asked to consider if the CCA is still relevant in what is a completely different media age from the one that existed when it first came on to the statute book.

You may also be invited to examine the working relationship between the Attorney General, in whose name any contempt proceedings against the media will be instituted, and the media. The Attorney General issues guidance to editors, usually reminding them of the contempt legislation (as if they needed reminding!) and their obligations under the law. This usually occurs when the police are investigating a particularly sensitive matter and the Attorney General is concerned that 'extravagant' reporting may prejudice any forthcoming trial or a trial that is actually under way. The most serious potentially prejudicial reporting in recent years was that associated with the Soham murders, for which Ian Huntley was found guilty at the Old Bailey in late 2003.

From contempt, the course will probably evolve into an examination of the section 10 provision of the CCA. The topic will usually be entitled 'protection of sources'. It is deemed by the media to be a fundamental principle that journalists should do everything possible to protect the sources of their information. The assumption is that if those who supply the media with information should have their identities exposed, then the stream of stories would ultimately dry up. This would mean that numerous public interest exposés would never see the light of day. The view is supported by section 10 of the Act, which states (and you must learn this):

> No court may require a person to disclose, nor is any person guilty of contempt of court for refusing to disclose, the source of information contained in a publication for which he is responsible, unless it is established to the satisfaction of the court that the disclosure is necessary in the interest of justice or national security or for the prevention of disorder or crime.

It will be apparent that the words to be placed under the microscope are:

> that the disclosure is necessary

You will be expected to discuss when journalists would be under a legal obligation to disclose the identity of their sources. There is quite a large body of case law that has built up around the topic, not to mention the implications of the Hutton inquiry in 2004, when the BBC clearly tried to protect the source of the information concerning the issue of weapons of mass destruction that led to the disputed broadcast on the *Today* programme.

Allied to the question of protecting *sources* is the need to protect *information* on which stories are based. This could be listed as a subcategory of the 'protecting sources' topic. Journalists and broadcasters may be in possession of information that the authorities are keen to obtain. There may appear to be legitimate reasons, such as investigating serious crimes. Journalists are unlikely to hand over such information willingly. Therefore, the police or security services may resort to legal action to obtain the information. The question for you will be, 'Can – and, if so, how – may journalists resist such an application?' Therefore, knowledge of the relevant sections of the key legislation is important to your studies. The major acts are:

- Police and Criminal Evidence Act 1984
- Police Act 1997
- Official Secrets Act 1989
- Regulation of Investigatory Powers Act 2000
- Terrorism Act 2000
- Terrorism Act 2006.

The question that will probably be asked is, 'What impact do the increased powers to obtain journalistic material or even to force disclosure have on the right to free expression?' In other words, 'Is this legislation compatible with the terms of the Human Rights Act and the European Convention on Human Rights?'

The other obvious link is with section 10 of the CCA. If the alleged source of a leaked document is a crown servant, the government may use the *national security ground,* in section 10, in an endeavour to trace the source of the leak. An example that will be cited to you is the case of the *Secretary of State for Defence v. Guardian Newspapers [1985] AC 339.* In this case, a government employee had leaked information to *The Guardian* newspaper. The government wished to identify the source. The leak was in the form of a photocopy of a secret Ministry of Defence document relating to the utilisation and location of Cruise missiles in the UK. The government requested the return of the photocopied document in an attempt to identify the source of the leak. *The Guardian* acknowledged that if the photocopy were returned, then it was likely that the source would be identified. The House of Lords, by a majority of three to two, ordered the document to be returned on the basis of the national security ground in section 10. The reasoning accepted by the majority was that the government needed to identify the source because she (as it transpired) was a potential source of further leaks and could jeopardise national security. So, the request was for a document, not a name. *The Guardian* did not know the name of the source. After the document was returned, the source was identified and prosecuted under the Official Secrets Act and sentenced to six months in prison.

Moving on from sources, I suspect the next topic will be privacy and breach of confidentiality. A journalist could try to maintain that his relationship with his source should, in law, be viewed as confidential in the same way that the law views relationships such as:

- doctor/patient
- lawyer/client
- priest/penitent.

This topic is one that is almost certain to appear on examination papers. This is because of the more recent case law developments and the open-ended question, at least for the moment, as to whether or not this country is on the brink of recognising, for the first time, a discrete body of law labelled 'privacy'. Arguably, the judges have stretched the law on confidence as far as possible and the incorporation of Article 8 of the Convention on Human Rights via the Human Rights Act 1998 into our law means that this development is now more than a distinct possibility. The government has always shown a marked reluctance to promote legislation, probably for fear of being accused of limiting press freedom in the name of privacy.

This topic is likely to be examined in two parts. The first is the law on confidence and there will be two themes. The first will be a brief historical analysis of the law dating back to the seminal decision in *Prince Albert v. Strange [1849] 64 ER 293* (more on this later). The second will be how the courts have 'stretched' the law on confidence almost to breaking point over the last decade. The situation was recognised and acknowledged by the Court of Appeal in *Douglas & Another v. Northern and Shell PLC & Another [2000] EWCA Civ 353* (para 88):

> *The Commission appears to be saying that, since the authorities in this country have been content to leave it to the judges to develop the law in this sensitive field, it is the judges who must develop the law so that it gives appropriate recognition to Article 8(1) rights. Whether they do so in the future by an extension of the existing frontiers of the law of confidence or by recognising the existence of new relationships which give rise to enforceable legal rights ... is not for this court, on this occasion to predict.*

It is possible that you may face a question in an examination about whether or not it is possible to stretch the law of confidence any further and, if so, whether or not it would be far enough to encompass Article 8 rights. Logic will tell you that there has to be judicial recognition of a new jurisprudence based Article 8 and the concomitant rights of privacy that will be developed by the court. What is not known at the moment is whether those remedies will be seen purely within the context of the Human Rights Act or the judges will develop a new tort of privacy with an ambit wider than the 1998 Act.

The second part will be to focus purely on the word privacy. Do we now have a new species of tort called privacy? What will be the implications of the *Caroline* case decision if adopted by the English courts? Why didn't the House of Lords go further in the *Naomi Campbell* case towards recognising privacy as a tort in its own right? What are the 'politics' behind the judicial refusal to take the quantum leap and recognise a new tort or, looked at from another angle, why is the government reluctant to legislate in favour of a law on privacy? These are some of the issues we will look at later.

The above topics are likely to consume something like 70 per cent of your academic year, depending, of course, on how it is structured. If you work within the context of a semester system, then I would be very surprised if this subject were a one-semester module – there is simply too much material to cover in ten or eleven weeks without making the course pretty superficial. So, let us assume that the media law course will be taught over two semesters, the major topics are those outlined above and so your tutor will then have to decide which other elements to choose to keep you occupied for the rest of the time.

There is a reasonable chance that you will have to look at the *regulatory framework* within which the UK media has to operate. Here you will consider, for the print media, the role of the Press Complaints Commission and, for broadcasting, the Office of Communications, (Ofcom). You will have to point out that the former is an industry body and that will lead you to question its impartiality. However, it has an adjudication process that attracts a not insignificant number of applications each year. Its Code of Practice is updated annually, taking into account any severe criticism of the media's conduct in the previous year. The code does lay down the framework within which journalists are expected to operate. Its weakness is that it does not provide financial compensation for those who have their complaints upheld. Tutors would include this in the syllabus, simply to make you aware that there are avenues other than the judicial to follow if you have a complaint but don't feel that the media's actions warrant taking legal action.

Broadcasting regulation is carried out by Ofcom – a regulatory body that was set up under the Communications Act 2003 and has been operational since December of that year. It took over the responsibilities of what are now referred to as the 'legacy regulators' – the five organisations that had previously regulated broadcasting. They were the:

- Broadcasting Standards Commission
- Independent Television Commission
- Radio Authority
- Office of Telecommunications (Oftel)
- Radio Communications Agency.

The former codes of practice are now redundant as a new Broadcasting Code came into effect in July 2005. The new code was produced taking into account the relevant provisions of the Human Rights Act 1998. The full text of the code is available via the Ofcom website (at www.ofcom.org.uk).

Perhaps it is just worth noting here that Parliament agreed that complaints about advertising on television and radio are to be dealt with by the Advertising Standards Authority rather than Ofcom.

It will be up to your tutor to decide how far to delve into the regulatory framework. My guess is that the focus will be on the regulatory bodies and the role of self-regulation within the framework of freedom of expression for the media.

Broadcasting regulation is multidimensional, in the sense that UK broadcasting is influenced by:

- legislation, such as the Broadcasting Act 1996
- European directives, such as the Television Without Frontiers Directive (still under discussion at the time of writing)
- European competition law
- the Broadcasting Code, but do note that, mainly for historical reasons, the BBC is not subject to much of the 2005 code (the provisions relating to the BBC are to be found in the its editorial guidelines, accessible at *www.bbc.co.uk*).

Notwithstanding, this topic can be expanded to include an investigation into the concept of public service broadcasting because of the unique position in world broadcasting of the BBC and its funding mechanism, by a national licence fee. Public service broadcasters do have a special position in the European Union, but, when running costs are funded by a licence fee, then elements of European competition law surface. The question is, 'Does the income generated from the fees constitute state aid and put these broadcasters at an advantage by comparison with private-sector providers of television and radio services?' This issue has surfaced recently as part of the charter review process for the BBC. You may also wish to consider the Ofcom PSB review undertaken in 2005 (this can be accessed at www.ofcom.org.uk by typing 'PSB review 2005' into the search engine on the home page).

The other major dimension of this is to look outside the UK and examine broadcasting regulation within a European context. Article 10 of the European Convention on Human Rights applies throughout the European Union, but each country comes to the table with very different broadcasting environments. This could also figure in the introductory part of your course, when considering freedom of expression as European broadcasting may be taken as a minicase study.

In December 2005, a new draft of the EU Television Without Frontiers Directive was published. This is meant to reflect the rapid technological changes that are taking place in the European audiovisual sector. Once implemented, there will be a dramatic change in the way that advertising is controlled. The result is likely to be more sponsored advertising and, for the first time, product placement will be defined and granted a clear legal framework.

Another related topic that may arise is that of *copyright* and *image rights*. In other words, a brief examination of two elements of intellectual *property law*. This can only be a superficial look at the law in recognition of the fact that the law on copyright is extremely complex. The major piece of legislation is the Copyright, Designs and Patents Act 1988, which extends to over 300 sections!

A visit to your local newsagents or supermarket will expose you to a plethora of magazines, seemingly covering every conceivable topic, from gardens to gigabytes, cooking to health and, of course, the daily diet of celebrity exposés. The content of many of these magazines will be photographic with text a poor second. The images that we see have a value. Photographic agencies regularly engage in media auctions in order to sell to the highest bidder, but what of the celebrities who are caught on camera?

From a legal point of view, if the celebrity has agreed to be photographed and received a fee, that will be the end of the matter. The relationship between the photographer and subject will then be regulated by contract. What, though, of the images of celebrities taken in public places? Those images have a potential commercial value to the photographer, magazine or newspaper or all three. The celebrity has nothing other than the dubious honour of being caught in an offguard moment. Should the law protect the celebrity's image rights?

At the moment, there is no discrete body of law entitled 'image rights' and so aggrieved celebrities are seeking to exploit other established areas of law in order to achieve recompense. These areas include *passing off*, *trademarks* and, of course, *copyright*. Add to this the current situation with regard to privacy as a result of the *Caroline* case and it will be obvious why this topic may well surface in your media law course.

However, as I said earlier, it can only be a superficial examination of the law and will, in all probability, be targeted at particular issues, very often following on from a recently decided case.

Another topic that is likely to have a greater degree of prominence for the next couple of years at least is the *Freedom of Information Act 2000*. This legislation has been on the statute books for seven years but only came into effect on 1 January 2005, preceded by much frenetic activity as organisations, particularly public bodies, prepared for its implementation. The preparation seems to have been crushed into the four months immediately preceding the implementation rather than the four years intended when the legislation went on to the statute book.

The Act applies to central and local government, the police, universities, schools and the armed forces, although, as might be expected, not the security services, nor the courts. It also covers the myriad of quangos we have created in this country, together with Parliament and the assemblies of Wales and Northern Ireland. Publicly owned companies are also covered. In all, it is estimated that some 100,000 public authorities are covered by the Act.

Trainee journalists are perhaps more likely than undergraduates to have this topic included as part of their training programme as they will need to know in some detail how to gain maximum benefit from the legislation once they have qualified. If you are a trainee journalist, then, you should become familiar with how to request information. All these organisations will have freedom of information officers, to whom requests for information should be sent. You should also familiarise yourself with the exemptions specified by the Act. You will not be entitled to have access to court documents or security-related information. If the provisions of the Data Protection Act 1998 are likely to be breached, then you will not be able to obtain personal data about individuals.

The provision that is likely to be of most practical interest to you is the *duty/public interest test*. This means that, in challenging a decision, you will have to show that the public interest served by disclosure is *greater* than the public interest served by confidentiality. You might well use this in relation to information that might prejudice:

- defence
- commercial interests
- the effective conduct of public affairs
- international relations
- the economic and financial interest of the UK
- law enforcement.

This will be a fertile area for interpretation and it can be expected that a list of precedents will soon be created.

The full list of exemptions is contained in Part II of the Act.

The above topics represent the major areas for consideration, assessment and examination. There are others that may be included as whole or part topics, such as *censorship*. This could well be a subdivision of the discussion regarding media regulation, as the various broadcasting codes have provisions relating to apparent 'good taste'. You may already be aware of the 9 p.m. 'watershed', before which broadcasters need to be circumspect about what is transmitted – more 'adult' or 'mature' content needing to appear *after* 9 p.m. The transmission by BBC2 of the musical *Jerry Springer: The Opera* in 2005, regarded by many people as blasphemous, was screened after 10 p.m. on a Saturday night and prompted thousands to complain to the BBC – albeit the vast majority doing so before the programme was even broadcast!

I will now go into a little more detail about each of the above topics and endeavour to identify the issues you will be expected to understand and discuss in the assessment process.

From the outset of the course, assess the weighting to be given to each topic on the syllabus. The greater the amount there is to discuss, the more likely it is that there will be a question in the examination on that topic. If there is a lot of recent case law or a new piece of legislation has been introduced, once again you are likely to have an examination question dealing with the issue.

2.3	
introductory themes	

Core Areas

- Freedom of expression
- Public interest

Before embarking on this section, please re-read my comments at the beginning of this chapter, where I suggested that an introduction to media law would, in all probability, centre on concepts such as free speech, and its links with human rights and constitutional and legislative rights, and the emotive concept of public interest.

It is in this early part of the course that you could be introduced to the law *against prior restraint.* If you are reading media law as a media studies undergraduate or a trainee journalist without prior legal knowledge, then you are also likely to be briefly introduced to the major elements of the English legal system (see pages 21 and 168).

Freedom of expression

To ease yourself into this introductory segment of the course, you may care to consult Ian Hargreaves' book entitled *Journalism: Truth or Dare*

(Oxford University Press, 2003). In assessing the challenges facing journalists in the twenty-first century, he wonders aloud if the constitutional privileges accorded to press freedom can be justified. In the introduction, he quotes Dr Onora O'Neill's 2002 Reith Lectures and it would be advantageous for you to look at the phrase 'free expression', as she does, as being, for your purposes at least, a synonym for 'press freedom'. Dr O'Neill's lectures can be found on the BBC's website at www.bbc.co.uk/print/radio4/reith2002, but the following extracts from the fifth lecture are to the point and useful to quote in coursework assignments:

> Outstanding reporting and accurate writing mingle with editing and reporting that smears, sneers and jeers, names, shames and blames. Some reporting 'covers' (or should I say 'uncovers'?) dementing amounts of trivia, some misrepresents, some denigrates, some teeters on the brink of defamation. In this curious world, commitments to trustworthy reporting are erratic: there is no shame in writing on matters beyond a reporter's competence, in coining misleading headlines, in omitting matters of public interest or importance, or in recirculating others' speculations as supposed 'news'. Above all there is no requirement to make evidence accessible to readers.

So, what's the solution? As she says later on in the fifth lecture:

> We may use twenty-first century communication technologies, but we still cherish nineteenth-century views of freedom of the press, above all those of John Stuart Mill. The wonderful image of a free press speaking the truth to power and that of investigative journalists as tribunes of the people belong to those more dangerous and heroic times. In democracies the image is obsolescent: journalists face little danger (except on overseas assignments) and the press do not risk being closed down. On the contrary, the press has acquired unaccountable power that others cannot match ... the classic arguments for press freedom do not endorse, let alone require, a press with unaccountable power. A free press can be and should be an accountable press ... Like Mill we may be passionate about individual freedom of expression, and so about the freedom of the press to represent individual's opinions and views. But freedom of expression is for individuals, not for institutions. We have good reasons for allowing individuals to express opinions even if they are invented, false, silly, irrelevant or plain crazy, but hardly for allowing powerful institutions to do so.

So, there you have it in a nutshell. The fourth estate is powerful and influential. What exactly does freedom of expression – a fundamental principle seeped in nineteenth-century political writing – actually mean in the twenty-first century? In terms of your analysis, to quote the above (or something similar) should gain you credit because you are not looking at the principle in isolation. You will need to consider that John Stuart Mill's argument, expounded in his treatise *On Liberty*, which was that freedom of expression is fundamental to *political freedom*, is only one aspect of the argument. He strongly condemns any attempt to stifle free expression in that the views not expressed will mean that there is a 'loss' to the human race. Progress will be slowed, education will be diminished and truth will be tarnished.

For a more detailed analysis of the principle of freedom of speech argued from a theoretical and practical perspective, see Eric Barendt's *Freedom of Speech* (Oxford University Press, 2005 (2nd ed.)). He states that:

> Written constitutions and bills of rights invariably protect freedom of speech as one of the fundamental liberties guaranteed against state suppression ... there is probably widespread public support for the free speech principle.

Contrast those words with the following from Amanda Russell and Margaret Smillie at the eighteenth BILETA Conference at Queen Mary and Westfield College of the University of London in April 2003:

> Freedom of expression has long been held to be the cornerstone of a democratic society. Historically it was one of the first human rights to be demanded and indeed to be guaranteed in law whether constitutionally, as in the US, or by judicial enactment, as in the UK. The press in particular has received special constitutional guarantees throughout the world, in particular against censorship.

Be aware of the four free speech theories advocated by Barendt. The first is the argument associated with John Stuart Mill, that free speech means open discussion, which in turn leads to the discovery of the truth. (Query whether the discovery of truth is always to be welcomed or not.) The second theory is that free speech is seen 'as an integral aspect of each individual's right to self-development and fulfilment'. If a person is inhibited in what can be written or spoken, then this will inhibit the growth of his or her personality. The third theory is, as Barendt says, 'probably the most, and certainly the most fashionable, easily understandable, free speech theory in modern Western democracies'. It is that free speech encourages the development of, and participation in, democratic values and institutions. The most obvious of these is having the right to vote in an election and exercising that right. The fourth is the idea that free speech counteracts any tendency by government to limit 'radical or subrersive ideas'.

So, in your introduction to media law via the medium of an assessment of the principle of free speech, the above represent some of the theoretical arguments you will come across placed in a practical context.

However, that is not the end of your involvement. At no stage have we referred to any constitutional documents or judicial pronouncements. The constitutional documents most likely to be referred to are the Constitution of the USA and the European Convention on Human Rights. You will be asked to consider the 1st Amendment to the Constitution with Article 10 of the Convention. Once you have become familiar with their terms, you should move on to judicial comments in an endeavour to illustrate how the courts have interpreted the documents. Try to identify a recent judgment as that will prevent an examiner from posing the question 'Is that still the case now?' So, by way of illustration, you could use the case of *Murphy v. Ireland [2003] ECHR 352.*

Remember that you are not dealing with this case from the point of view of the substantive issues, but, rather, using quotes from the court regarding Article 10. In para. 65, the court said:

> The Court recalls that freedom of expression constitutes one of the essential foundations of a democratic society [but] ... the exercise of that freedom carries with it duties and responsibilities. No restriction on freedom of expression, whether in the context of religious beliefs or in any other, can be compatible with Article 10 unless it satisfies, inter alia, the test of necessity as required by the second paragraph of that article.

You must always look at the European Court of Human Rights' website (at www.echr.coe.int) because, I assure you, there will be no shortage of cases involving adjudications of Article 10. You will therefore continue to find that the recent judicial thinking on Article 10 is readily available there. An example, at the time of writing, is the case of *Selistö v. Finland [2004] ECHR 634.*

In para. 46 of the judgment, the Court states:

> According to the Court's well-established case law, freedom of expression constitutes one of the essential foundations of a democratic society and one of the basic conditions for its progress and each individual's self-fulfilment.

This is a most useful statement from a student's perspective because it allows you to comment on the link between the three theories advocated by Barendt and the above statement by the Court. Here there is a clear reference to the second and third theories (see Part Four for a case note).

All that remains in terms of introductory material is to mention the Constitution of the USA and the 1st Amendment. The Supreme Court has the power to strike down state and federal legislation that conflicts with the Constitution. Perhaps the most famous case to which you will be referred is _The New York Times v. Sullivan [1964]_. It is often referred to as a landmark decision, the importance of which is hard to overestimate. The decision by the Supreme Court that established actual malice had to be proved before press reports could be considered defamatory meant that the civil rights campaign in the southern states could be freely reported. It is widely regarded as one of the key decisions supporting freedom of the press. It means that the press cannot be sued for libel unless the publisher knows that a statement is false or acts with reckless disregard for the truth.

To fully appreciate the significance of this decision, you need to know that, at the time, there were libel suits outstanding against news organisations from the southern states to the tune of $300 million. As you can imagine, this caused many newspapers to exercise great caution when reporting civil rights issues. Public officials would be all too ready to claim that they had been libelled if newspapers attacked the policies of the politicians or actions of the police when monitoring civil rights events. After the decision, the media was free to report the widespread disorder and civil rights infringements that occurred. _The New York Times_ had maintained that the actions brought against news organisations were vexatious and designed to intimidate them into refusing to report civil unrest as the southern states in particular sought to maintain segregation.

Public interest

A logical starting place when investigating the public interest concept is the Press Complaints Commissions's Code of Practice. Although having no legal force, it does purport to define 'public interest', at least from a journalistic viewpoint. It states:

1   _The public interest includes, but is not confined to:_

   i) detecting or exposing crime or serious impropriety
   ii) protecting public health and safety
   iii) preventing the public from being misled by an action or statement of an individual or organisation.

2   *There is a public interest in freedom of expression itself.*
3   *Whenever the public interest is invoked, the PCC will require editors to demonstrate fully how the public interest was served.*
4   *The PCC will consider the extent to which material is already in the public domain or will become so.*
5   *In cases involving children under 16, editors must demonstrate an exceptional public interest to override the normally paramount interest of the child.*

So there are several factors, viewed from an industry standpoint, as to what amounts to the public interest. The expectation is that this interpretation will accord with judicial thinking, otherwise there is tremendous potential for conflict.

Always consider whether the industry's perception of a particular term or phrase accords with that of the judiciary. The media will constantly call to its aid the concept of public interest as a means of justifying a course of action.

You would be right if you expected that this term has been the subject of much judicial comment. Therefore, as you progress through the course, simply make notes on cases in which the words have been commented on or defined. One example has already been given – that of *Lion Laboratories v. Evans [1984]*. Here is an example of the kinds of notes you could make about this case.

Topic: public interest

Prior to *Lion Laboratories*

1   See Lord Denning's comments in *Schering Chemicals Ltd v. Falkman Ltd [1981] 2 All ER 321*. Public interest equated with freedom of the press, only to be curtailed 'when there is a substantial risk of grave injustice'. (prior restraint case.)
2   See Lord Denning in *Woodward v. Hutchins [1977] 2 All ER 751*. Here, balancing the public interest of maintaining a confidence against the public interest of knowing the truth.
3   See Sir John Donaldson in *Francome v. Mirror Newspapers [1984] 2 All ER 408*. Media 'vulnerable' to confusing the public interest with their own interest. 'Usually these march hand in hand, but not always.'

Post *Lion Laboratories*

4   See Rose J in *X. v. Y. [1988] 2 All ER 648.* Public interest of preserving confidentiality of hospital records identifying AIDS sufferers outweighed the public interest of the freedom of the press to publish the information.

5   See Sir Stephen Brown P in *W. v. Egdell [1990] 1 All ER 835.* Balance of public interest lay in disclosure of 'vital information' to the Secretary of State who had the onerous duty of safeguarding public safety.

The above is simply an illustration of how a chronological approach helps to determine if there have been any significant changes in how judges assess public interest. You will see that, in many cases, it is not just simply a matter of deciding if there is a public interest defence but also involves determining which of two public interest issues takes precedence. You will also have noticed that discussion as to where the public interest lies frequently arises when there has been an alleged breach of confidence.

Here is an example of notes made on recent cases in this area.

Latest public interest cases

1   *A v. B & C [2002] EWCA Civ 337* Lord Woolf CJ. Court not justified in interfering with the freedom of the press where there is *no* identifiable public interest served by any particular material being published. In the majority of situations, whether the public interest is involved or not will be obvious. (Injunctions and prior restraint.)

2   *Cream Holdings Ltd & Others v. Banerjee and Others [2004]* UKHL44. Lord Nicholls: 'The principal matter the *Echo* wishes to publish is "incontestably" a matter of serious public interest ... the story was one ... no court could properly suppress. (Prior restraint.)

3   *Campbell v. MGN Ltd [2004] UKHL22* Accepted that it was in the public interest to correct the record on Campbell's drug taking after previous denials, but not to publish photographs of her attending a drug rehabilitation centre. (Privacy.)

4   *McKennitt v. Ash [2006] EWHC 3003 (QB).* Where the public interest lies when Articles 8 and 10 are in conflict. (Privacy.)

I do not for one moment want to claim that the above represents a comprehensive list of public interest cases. My purpose here is simply to illustrate how you can save yourself an enormous amount of work by simply extracting a few choice comments from the law reports and noting them as you proceed through the course. They act as a useful aide-memoire when it comes to commencing revision later in the year. Remember, the media will use the public interest as a defence in actions for defamation and, in particular, when wishing to publish confidential material and oppose applications for injunctions prior to publication.

2.4	
defamation	

Core Areas

- Definition of defamation
- Do the words relate to the claimant?
- Every fresh publication of an allegedly defamatory statement may give rise to a fresh cause of action
- what kinds of comments may be held to be defamatory?
- Defences in defamation actions

This is a major topic and you are certain to have to answer questions on it that involves a number of different aspects of the law. There are so many issues that you may be given the opportunity to deliver a coursework essay on the topic as well as a problem question in the examination.

I will go through the key elements of this subject as succinctly as possible.

Introductory comments

You need to understand and appreciate the significance of the following.

- The distinction between the terms *libel* and *slander*. The basic distinction is that libel relates to the *written* word and slander to the *spoken* word. A better view is that the former should be assumed to refer to anything that is in permanent, or at least non-transient, form. You should also take a passing interest in the tort of *malicious falsehood* as an alternative action to that of defamation. When dealing with the distinction, although arguably there is no real justification today for its maintenance, note that, under provisions of the Defamation Act 1996 and the Broadcasting Act 1990, defamatory statements broadcast on radio and television will be viewed as libel, not slander. The assumption is that, as broadcasts are automatically recorded, then the words exist in a permanent form. Having said that, the Theatres Act 1968 makes defamatory words spoken at public performances libel!

- Note that libel is actionable, as the lawyers say, per se. In simple terms, that means without proof of any special damage occurring as a result of the defamatory words. The opposite is true for slander, subject to four specific exceptions. An example, would be an actor who suddenly finds that his work in the theatre has dried up because of the allegedly defamatory comments.
- Please remember that, for a claimant to take the proceedings all the way to the High Court, this is invariably an action of last resort. There is little incentive to bring such an action as Legal Aid is not available and the Defamation Act 1996 introduced other ways in which an alleged attack on someone's reputation could be resolved. Please note, too, the offer of amends provisions in sections 2–4. As a result of the decisions in *Nail v. News Group Newspapers & Others [2004] EWCA Civ 1708, Milne v. Express Newspapers PLC [2004] EWCA Civ 664 [2004] EMLR 24, Campbell-James v. Guardian Media Group [2005] EWHC 893* and *Turner v. News Group Newspapers [2006] EWCA Civ 540*, it is possible that a question on the offer of amends may be asked in forthcoming examinations (see Part Four for details of some of these cases).

  You should also note the *summary procedure* in sections 8–10.
- In many cases, all a claimant requires is for the record to be put right. Once again, when looking at a set of facts that make up a problem question, you can score heavily at the beginning of your answer if you make the point that there are alternatives to a full trial for the action.

By way of an introduction to a defamation question, make the point that the system is set up to filter actions away from a full trial. Only those with large chequebooks and, usually, correspondingly large egos will pursue an action all the way to the High Court and full trial.

- Two further points usually need to be emphasised by students. The first is that a High Court action in a defamation trial invariably involves a jury making the final decision on whether or not the claimant has succeeded. On occasions, a judge will sit without a jury if it is believed that the details would be too complex or technical for a jury, such as in George Galloway MP's libel action against *The Daily Telegraph* in November 2004. The second point concerns the role of the judge and jury. The judge will rule whether or not there is a case to go to trial and will advise the jury on the evidence. However, while the judge may decide that the words complained of are *capable* of being construed as defamatory, it is the jury that must decide whether or not they *are*. The judge will also advise the jury on the amount that they ought to consider awarding by way of damages should they find for the claimant. In the past, juries had literally an unfettered discretion on the amount to award and this led to huge sums being given to claimants. You should become familiar with a couple of cases by way of illustration. Here are two good examples.

- *Sutcliffe v. Pressdram Ltd [1990] 1 All ER 269,* in which the wife of the 'Yorkshire Ripper' was awarded £600,000 damages to be paid by *Private Eye* (subsequently reduced to £60,000 plus interest).
- *Rantzen v. Mirror Group Newspapers [1993] 4 All ER 975,* in which television personality Esther Rantzen was awarded £250,000, but that was subsequently reduced to £110,000.

- The current situation is that courts do not wish the awards to be so large as to have a 'chilling effect' on journalism, bearing in mind the Article 10 right of freedom of expression. The upper limit of £200,000 suggested by judges to juries is now in line with personal injury awards. The highest award in 2003 was £65,000. You should, though, point out that, in very serious cases, awards of £200,000 have been made, with the judge suggesting that if he could have gone higher, then he would have done (see *Lillie & Reed v. Newcastle City Council [2002] EWHC 1600 (QB)*. In the *Galloway* case, the damages were set at £150,000, although in this the judge sat alone. However, juries do occasionally go beyond the guidelines suggested by the judges. In October 2005, Rupert Lowe, Chairman of Southampton Football Club, was awarded £250,000 in damages after *The Times* accused him of treating a former manager of the club 'shabbily'. In May 2006, the jury in *Purnell v. Business F1 Magazine* awarded the claimant £75,000, despite Gray J advising them that the award ought to have been in the region of £25,000–£60,000.

Definition of defamation

Perhaps the definition quoted most often is that given by Lord Atkin in the House of Lords in the case of *Sim v. Stretch [1936] 2 All ER 1237*. This, or a variation on it, has seemingly been quoted in almost every defamation action since then. He said that defamation is:

A statement which tends to lower the claimant in the estimation of right-thinking members of society generally, and in particular to cause him to be regarded with feelings of hatred, contempt, ridicule, fear and disesteem.

The Faulks Committee on Defamation in 1975 came up with something similar:

> Defamation shall consist of a publication to a third party of matter which in all the circumstances would be likely to affect a person adversely in the estimation of reasonable people generally.

The critical question is whether or not the words referred to in a case are capable of carrying the defamatory meaning alleged. A case that is often cited to help answer this question is *Gillick v. British Broadcasting Corporation [1996] EMLR 267*. In the judgement for this case the law was summarised thus:

- the court should give to the material complained of the natural and ordinary meaning that it would have conveyed to the ordinary reasonable viewer watching the programme
- the hypothetical reasonable reader or viewer is not naive, nor unduly suspicious – he can 'read between the lines'; he can read in an implication but must not be treated as a man who is avid for scandal
- the court should be cautious of an over-elaborate analysis of the material issue and should not take too literal an approach.

The Court of Appeal has also approved the statement of Lord Morris in *Jones v. Skelton (1963) 1 WLR 1362*, which was to the effect that:

> In deciding whether words are capable of conveying a defamatory meaning, the court will reject those meanings which can only emerge as the product of some strained or forced or utterly unreasonable interpretation.

These are the sorts of statements you should quote in coursework and you must mention the gist of them in examination answers. For a recent endorsement of the 'reasonable or hypothetical viewer or reader' test, see *Charman v. Orion Publishing No 2 [2005] EWHC 2187 (QB)*, paras 9 and 10.

Always bear in mind that you should check the most recent cases to see if these statements are still being cited in the courts.

Do the words relate to the claimant?

It probably goes without saying, but the defamatory allegations must have been made about the claimant. If the person is expressly named, there is no problem, as in 'David Beckham, who was the captain of the

England football team'. Here, we are made doubly sure who the subject is. There may well be other people called David Beckham, but only one was the captain of England. In law, every person is deemed to have a valuable reputation unless the contrary can be proved.

You have to point out to your examiners that the test is whether or not the reasonable reader or viewer would associate the alleged defamatory comments with the claimant. The 'reasonable reader' could be anyone in the world or a limited number of people. The defamatory words must be 'published' to a third party. Often a newspaper will not specifically name the subject of an article, but, nevertheless, if there is sufficient information published to allow people to identify the person, that is enough.

It is worth noting that section 1 of the Defamation Act 1996 establishes a defence of 'innocent defamation', *providing* the person relying on this defence is not the author, editor or publisher. The point of the section is the recognition that other parties are usually involved in the dissemination of the defamatory piece, such as the printer of a magazine, distributors and newsagents. The defence is based on the person being able to show that he or she took reasonable care and did not know, and had no reason to believe, that what he or she did caused or contributed to the publication of a defamatory statement.

Take a look also at section 1(2) of the Defamation Act, because this provides definitions of 'author,' 'editor' and 'publisher'.

If you are a trainee journalist, the practical advice is to present as much accurate information as possible in order to avoid unintentional defamation. If it does occur, the newspaper should print a correction in a prominent part of the newspaper as soon as possible after the event. That would not necessarily mean an end to legal action, but it would make it more difficult for a claimant to prove that their reputation had been adversely affected.

Examiners love to use 'everyday' names in their problem questions. If you are reporting from Cardiff Crown Court and a Tom Jones has been found guilty of grievous bodily harm, it is incumbent on you to give enough information about him to ensure that there is no possible confusion with Tom Jones the pop star.

Every fresh publication of an allegedly defamatory statement may give rise to a fresh cause of action

Newspapers will sometimes carry a story that has been put into the public domain by a rival publication. A person may have been told something and he or she passes that on to colleagues or friends, who in turn tell others. Assuming that the story in the first instance was defamatory, those repeating the story are also at risk of defamation. In the Jimmy Nail case mentioned above in the introductory comments, the defendants were not only News Group Newspapers but also the Editor of the *News of the World,* Rebekah Wade, Jules Stenson, the journalist who wrote the story, Geraint Jones, the author of the book, and HarperCollins, his publishers.

When it was alleged in 2003 that Nicole Kidman had had an affair with Jude Law and this had led to his marriage breakdown, she successfully sued a number of newspapers after *The Sun* first and then the *Daily Mail* and *Sunday Telegraph* repeated the allegations. Examiners will want you to be aware of the *repetition rule.* In simple language, a new 'publication' comes into existence each time a defamatory remark or comment is repeated, thus creating a new cause of action.

From a study viewpoint, you should attempt to discover a succinct and authoritative judicial definition that adequately describes the 'rule' so that you may use it to good effect in your examinations. The following is an example.

Lord Reid *in Lewis v. The Daily Telegraph [1964] AC234, p. 260*

> *Repeating someone else's libellous statement is just as bad as making the statement directly.*

When citing an authority from some time ago, it is important to ascertain whether or not it is still valid today. Therefore, you need to seek more recent judicial endorsement to establish that it is. In the above case, you might cite *Stern v. Piper [1997] QB 123* or *Mark v. Associated Newspapers Ltd [2002] EWCA Civ 772*, both of which quote this definition with approval.

You may also wish to illustrate the principle by citing an example contained in an appropriate case. A good example is this one from Lord Justice Simon Brown in *Mark v. Associated Newspapers [2002]:*

> *the rule accords with reality. If A says to B that C says that D is a scoundrel, B will think just as ill of D as if he heard the statement directly from C. It will be worse in part because there will be many more Bs, and in part because responsible newspapers do not generally repeat serious allegations unless they think there is something in them so that the very fact of publication carries a certain weight.*

An example of the dangers inherent in making potentially libellous comments when the press is in the vicinity is shown by the decision in

McManus & Others v. Beckham [2002] EWCA Civ 939 (see Part Four for more on this). As Bingham LJ said in *Slipper v. BBC [1991] 1 All ER 165,* and was quoted by Lord Justice Laws in *McManus* (para 29):

> defamatory statements are objectionable not least because of their propensity to percolate through underground channels and contaminate hidden springs.

This area of *onward* dissemination of potentially defamatory material is also relevant to the position of Internet service providers. (ISPs). This, at the time of writing, will be a favourite topic for examiners because of the increasing realisation of the vulnerability of ISPs to transmitting defamatory material, given the existence of over three billion websites. If this topic does arise, you need to investigate the following points.

- ISPs will be regarded as innocent publishers within the context of section 1(3) and can avail themselves of the protection offered by section 1(1)(a) of the Defamation Act 1996. In general terms, they will be viewed as 'secondary publishers'.
- However, that protection will *not* apply if the ISP has been informed, or has reason to believe, that defamatory material has been posted on a site and the ISP does not remove the offending words. By choosing to do nothing, the ISP is, in effect, associating itself with the defamatory material and a new cause of legal action being taken is established, this time not against the creator of the material but against the *disseminator.* This approach has recently been confirmed by the High Court in the case of *Bunt v. Tilley & Others [2006] EWHC 407 (QB).* The position of an ISP was deemed to be different from that of other disseminators of defamatory material. Only if the ISP had notice of the alleged defamation and did nothing would it cease to have section 1 protection (see Part Four for more details).
- You may then be asked by your tutors to consider the implications of this case together with the previous authority of *Godfrey v. Demon Internet [2001] QB 201* and draw conclusions as to the legal position of ISPs in light of each ruling.

With the current focus on the Internet, you may be questioned about *forum shopping.* This is the term applied to the decision by a claimant about which jurisdiction to bring his or her action to. This is particularly pertinent to the Internet because websites can be accessed from virtually any country in the world. The following represent the core cases and issues to discuss.

- Has the claimant established a reputation in the particular jurisdiction in which legal action is contemplated and how many hits were there on the site from within that jurisdiction? This is the Internet equivalent of asking how many newspapers were published within the jurisdiction and how many were actually bought? In *Shevill v. Presse Alliance SA [1996] AC 959*, the plaintiff had her home in Yorkshire and was defamed by an article in *France Soir*. The newspaper had a circulation of about 200,000 in France, but only 250 in the UK, with perhaps 10 being read in Yorkshire. Nevertheless, it was held by the European Court of Justice that a claimant could bring an action for defamation before the courts of each state in which the publication was distributed and the claimant had suffered damage. Remember that, in our jurisdiction, damage is *assumed* to occur, but this is not a matter that affects the *jurisdictional* issue.

- Examine the case of *Lewis & Others v. King [2004] EWCA Civ 1329* for an assessment of the current law (see Part Four).
- As the Court of Appeal relied on other cases in coming to its decision, you will need to also consider:

  - *Gutnik v. Dow Jones [2002] HCA 56*
  - *Spiliada Maritime Corporation v. Cansulex Ltd [1987] AC 460*
  - *Duke of Brunswick v. Harmer (1849) 14 QB 185*
  - *Berezovsky v. Michaels [2000] 1 WLR 1004.*

The *Duke of Brunswick* case is deemed to be the original authority for the proposition that each publication constitutes a separate tort, although an examination of the report will probably lead you to conclude that the Duke received extremely favourable treatment from the court! Nevertheless, the rule has survived even the advent of the Internet. To back up that comment, you could cite the Lord Chief Justice in *Lewis*:

> a defendant who publishes on the Web may at least in theory find himself vulnerable to multiple actions in different jurisdictions.
>
> So far, then, the Duke of Brunswick has survived the Internet, certainly in the High Court of Australia.

To illustrate the fact that the *Duke of Brunswick* decision lives on, you should read the Court of Appeal's decision in *Dow Jones & Co. Inc. v. Yousef Abdul Latif Jameel [2005] EWCA Civ 75*. Lord Phillips of Worth Maltravers MR, when considering the strength of the decision, commented in his judgment:

> We do not think that this decision can stand as authority for more than the proposition that each separate publication gives rise to a separate cause of action.

To put it positively, the decision stands as authority for the proposition that each separate publication gives rise to a separate cause of action, but little else!

Further reading on this topic

Law Commission (2002) *Defamation and the Internet: A Preliminary Investigation,* Scoping Study *No.2 at:* www.lawcom.gov.uk/does/defamation2.pdf

Ludbrook, Tim (2004) Defamation and the Internet', *Entertainment Law Review,* 15(7), p. 173.

What kinds of comments may be held to be defamatory?

The answer is that it is difficult to predict because, ultimately, it will be for a jury to decide whether or not the case succeeds. The judge may well have to determine, as a preliminary point, that the words are *capable* of being considered defamatory, but, eventually, the jury will decide if the words *are* defamatory. Occasionally, as we saw in the *Galloway* case, with the agreement of each party, the trial will proceed without a jury.

Clearly, in an examination question, you will have to scrutinise carefully the words deemed to be defamatory. You will need to point out that you do so on the basis that you possess the qualities of the 'ordinary reader or viewer' described by Neill LJ in *Gillick v. BBC (1996) EMLR 267.* You will need to acknowledge that times and attitudes change and what might have been defamatory years ago may not be considered defamatory today. For example, in 1959, the popular pianist Liberace sued the *Daily Mirror* after it wrote:

> He is the summit of sex, the pinnacle of the masculine, feminine and neuter ... This deadly, winking, sniggering, snuggling, chromium plated, scent impregnated, ice-flavoured heap of mother love.

It is unlikely that to suggest someone is homosexual today would elicit the same response from ordinary readers as it might have done in the late 1950s, when to engage in homosexual behaviour was a criminal offence. In December 2005, Robbie Williams accepted substantial damages over claims in *The People* newspaper and two magazines that he is secretly homosexual. In addition, the publishers agreed to print a suitable apology. The real issue in this day and age of civil partnerships is not whether or not someone is gay or bisexual, but if they are *deceiving* someone by keeping their sexuality secret. In the *Williams* case, it was argued that he was deceiving his public in a book about his life by stating that he only had sex with women.

Listed (briefly) below are some examples of words that have been considered defamatory.

- In *Cornwell v. Myskow & Others [1987] 2 All ER 504*, the *Sunday People* and its television reviewer had to pay the actress Charlotte Cornwell £10,000 in damages for this:

  As a middle-aged star, all Miss Cornwell has going for her is her age. She can't sing, her bum is too big and she has the sort of stage presence that jams lavatories. Worst she belongs to that arrogant and self-deluded school of acting which believes that if you leave off your make-up and shout a lot that's great acting. It's art. For a start dear, you look just as ugly with make-up on as without it.

- William Roache, who plays *Coronation Street*'s Ken Barlow, was found to have been libelled after *The Sun* newspaper called him 'boring.'
- The actress Diana Rigg accepted £38,000 in damages in 2003 for libel and breach of privacy after the *Daily Mail* portrayed her as a lonely, embittered woman who had a 'low regard' for British men and had left the UK to retire and live a reclusive existence in France.
- The British MP George Galloway won £150,000 in damages from *The Daily Telegraph* for suggesting he was in the pay of Saddam Hussein's regime and that his conduct was traitorous.
- Nicole Kidman received damages after *The Sun* newspaper wrongly stated that she was having an affair with the actor Jude Law. The publication of the article had 'caused her considerable embarrassment and distress', her lawyer told the court.
- Sharon Stone won substantial damages from the *Daily Mail* for its suggestion that she had neglected her four-year-old son by leaving him asleep in her car while she went on a dinner date.

Remember, *innuendo* and *implication* are just as powerful as expressly stated words when it comes to establishing defamation. However, the reasonable reader or viewer, according the *Gillick* case, can read 'between the lines', but he or she will not strive to import unreasonable or strained interpretations on the words.

Defamation is an attack on reputation, so, as part of any analysis of a problem, you will first have to assert that the claimant possesses a reputation capable of being damaged. In general terms, you may assume that certain categories of people will have a reputation. These will include lawyers, doctors, surgeons, accountants … possibly anyone who is deemed to exercise skill and judgement in carrying out their functions. For an example, see *Irving v. Penguin Books [2000] EWHC* QB *115,* where the defence of justification prevailed because the court found that Irving's reputation as a historian was discredited by reason of his denial of the Holocaust.

Be prepared to acknowledge that there may well be borderline cases where the judges themselves disagree on whether or not the words are capable of being defamatory. A good example to cite is the case of *Berkoff v. Burchill & Another [1996] 4 All ER 1008.* The claimant, who is a well-known actor, director and writer, sought damages for libel from Times Newspapers and the writer of the articles, Julie Burchill. He claimed that words in the articles were understood to mean that he was 'hideously ugly' and were defamatory in the sense that he would be exposed to ridicule and or would tend to cause people to shun and avoid him.

The judge ruled that the words *were* capable of being defamatory. The defendants appealed, arguing that, just because a statement might hurt feelings or cause annoyance, this was not relevant to the issue of whether or not they were defamatory. What was needed, they claimed, was injury to reputation.

It was held, by a 2:1 majority, that if a person's standing among other people was not diminished, then there could be no successful action for defamation. However, words *were* capable of being defamatory if they held him up to:

> contempt, scorn or ridicule or tended to exclude him from society, notwith-standing that they neither imputed disgraceful conduct to him nor any lack of skill or efficiency in his chosen profession.

You could use this quote for examination purposes to describe the meaning of defamation.

As a matter of good practice, if a decision is by a majority, then you should look at the reasoning of all the judges. The majority in the case above emphasised the importance of the context in which the words were published. Here was a man who made his living in part as an actor and the words were capable of suggesting that he was repulsive. Physical beauty may not be necessary if you are a writer or director, but it may of course be relevant to one's career as an actor. Millett LJ, the dissenting judge, offered hope to all ugly men by offering the following words of comfort:

> It is a common experience that ugly people have satisfactory social lives … and it is a popular belief for the truth of which I am unable to vouch that ugly men are particularly attractive to women.

Millett LJ professed that he could not take this claim seriously and even went so far as to apologise if he had treated the claim with 'unjudicial levity'. Nevertheless, he could not persuade his brethern to adopt his reasoning!

Examiners will also expect you to take account of words *and* any references to photographs in the facts they lay before you in a problem question. This means that they will expect you to consider the meaning as a whole. In all likelihood, this will mean introducing the concept of *bane and antidote*.

The leading case for this is *Charleston v. News Group Newspapers [1995] 2 All ER 313* (see Part Four for details). Judges believe that photographs can have a more enduring impact on a reader than text. In some cases, the text may be ignored altogether while readers take in the images, and possibly the headlines laid out graphically in front of them. The importance of reading the words is that they may *correct* the first impression gained from looking at the images. This is known as *bane and antidote*. *Bane* means 'the cause of ruin or trouble' and *antidote* means 'anything that counteracts something unpleasant or evil.' In other words, the evil of the images may be corrected by the words of the text.

A final point I wish to make before moving on to consider defences is to urge you to remember to look for hidden meanings or innuendo in the words you find in an examination question. An item can sometimes mean something that is not apparent from a straightforward reading or viewing of the material. Very often, in order for innuendo to succeed, the 'ordinary person' will need to be aware of some special circumstances or have particular knowledge. If a newspaper reports that a well-known MP is a regular visitor to number 20 Acacia Avenue, then the ordinary reader or viewer would probably think nothing of it, unless he or she knew that it was a brothel or a crack house.

An old example, but one often found in the modern books nevertheless, is *Cassidy v. Daily Mirror Newspapers Ltd [1929] 2 KB 331*. The *Daily Mirror* printed a photograph of a racehorse owner together with a young woman with a caption stating that they had just announced their engagement. Unfortunately, the gentleman concerned was already married. His wife brought an action claiming defamation in that those who knew her would think that she had been living in 'immoral cohabitation' and passing herself off as being married. It was held that the item was capable of being defamatory.

Defences in defamation actions

The major defences that you will be expected to discuss are:

- justification or truth
- fair comment
- privilege – absolute, qualified and common law qualified privilege.

However, do not forget that sections 2–4 of the Defamation Act 1996 introduced the offer of amends procedure. This permits the defendant to make a written offer to correct the libel and apologise or to publish a suitable correction. Damages will also have to be paid. There is a limitation, though, in that the defence will not apply where the defendant knew, or had reason to believe, the statement referred to the claimant and was false and defamatory of him or her. However, section 4(3) states that:

> it shall be presumed until the contrary is shown that he did not know and had no reason to believe that was the case.

Examiners will usually wish you to carry out an appraisal of the major defences and accompanying case law. When deciding by reference to a set of facts which, if any, defence is appropriate, do show that you realise how *difficult* a defence of justification will be to prove. Also, be prepared to indicate that the higher the sting appears in the *Lucas-Box* levels (for further details about the levels see the *Elaine Chase v. News Group Newspapers [2002]* case in Part Four), the more compelling the evidence will need to be to justify the allegation in the first place. The continued application of the *Lucas-Box* levels was recently endorsed by Eady J in *Fallon v. MGN Ltd (No. 2) [2006] EWHC 783 (QB)* (see para 1).

Justification

The basic proposition is that truth is a complete defence to any defamatory statement of fact.

The defence works by the defendants seeking to show that the allegation they are seeking to justify is overwhelmingly correct. Point out to your examiner that it is unnecessary to show that *every single* fact stated is correct (have regard to section 5 of the Defamation Act 1952). For example, if a journalist alleged that a well-known politician had sex with a prostitute at hotel X, when, in fact, it was at hotel Y, the defence would not be lost. Of course, this assumes that the politician *did* have sex with the prostitute and this can be *proved* to the satisfaction of the court. The other point you should emphasise is the *quality* of the evidence submitted to support the allegation. It should be clarified what evidence will be admissible to assist the defendants. For example, a source who is more than willing to provide information prior to publication may not be so keen to appear in the High Court to substantiate the claim months later. (Please consider the *Galloway* case report and consider why you believe *The Daily Telegraph* did not rely on justification as a defence for their charges against the MP.) An excellent recent example is the scathing comments of Eady J in *Purnell v. Business F1 Magazine Ltd & Another, 14 March 2006* (for the full text of the report, please visit 5rb's website at: *www.5rb.co.uk).* The comment from 5rb says it all:

> This is a rare example of a case where the evidence put forward by the defendants on justification is so weak that summary judgment is granted.

It is often assumed that by the simple expedient of putting the word 'alleged' in front of a statement, the writer or speaker cannot be sued if the statement is untrue. This may occur when a newspaper publishes what is, in fact, nothing more than a rumour. An examiner may put a similar issue to you in a problem. The fact that the *rumour* exists may well be true, but it does not mean that the rumour is *true.* Trainee journalists please take on board Lord Devlin's words in his judgment for the case of *Lewis v. The Daily Telegraph [1964] AC 234:*

> you cannot escape liability for defamation by putting the libel behind a prefix such as 'I have been told ...' or 'it is rumoured ...' and then asserting that it was true that you had been told or that it was in fact being rumoured.

You might care to use the following quotes from Eady J from his judgment for the *Galloway* case (paras 15 and 35, respectively) as neat commentaries on the law of justification:

> There is no plea of justification; that is to say, it is no part of the Defendant's case to allege that what they published was true in any sense that was defamatory of Mr Galloway ... I need to make clear that despite references in their submissions to a 'strong prima facie case' and to the desirability of a 'full investigation' the defendants do not allege that the words are true in the sense that there were 'reasonable grounds to suspect' or 'grounds to investigate'.

It is trite law that if a defendant asserts 'X says that Y has committed murder', he can only justify by proving that Y has committed murder. It does not avail him to prove merely that X had made the claim.

Fair comment

The basic idea underpinning the law relating to fair comment was summarised by Lord Nicholls of Birkenhead in the case of *Albert Cheng v. Tse Wai Chun Paul [2000] HKLRD 418*. He first alluded to the words 'fair comment' and thought them inaccurate, preferring instead 'Comment, or honest comment'. The title of the defence he thought 'misleading'. He then went on to detail five 'non-controversial' matters about the ingredients of the defence. These are:

- the comment must be on a matter of public interest and public interest is not to be confined within 'narrow limits'
- the comment must be 'recognisable as comment, as distinct from an imputation of fact'
- the comment must be based on facts that are true or protected by privilege: 'If the facts on which the comment purports to be founded are not proved to be true or published on a privileged occasion, the defence of fair comment is not available'
- the comment must 'explicitly or implicitly indicate, at least in general terms, what are the facts on which the comment is being made. The reader or hearer should be in a position to judge for himself how far the comment was well founded'
- the comment must be one which could have been made by an honest person, however prejudiced he might be, and however exaggerated or obstinate his views. It must be germane to the subject matter criticised. But a critic need not be mealy mouthed in denouncing what he disagrees with. He is entitled to dip his pen in gall for the purposes of legitimate criticism.'

Lord Nicholls described these five points as the 'outer limits' of the defence. The burden of proving that the defence falls within these limits rests with the *defendant*.

Examiners will create problems in which it will be difficult to separate fact and opinion. You might care to look at two cases to illustrate the point. In *Galloway MP v. Telegraph Group Ltd [2004] EWHC 2786 (QB)* Eady J concluded that there was 'no basis upon which the defence of fair comment can succeed.' Even though the words used by *The Daily Telegraph* were to be found in the leader column, a natural home for comment, the judge concluded that statements such as:

David Blair uncovered strong prima facie evidence that a British MP had been in the pay of a foreign dictator with whom this country had just been at war.

was not comment. It was, the judge said, 'A classic example of a defamatory assertion that is susceptible to a defence of justification.'

In *Branson v. Bower [2001] EWCA Civ 791,* Bower's article in the *Evening Standard* was judged by reference to what the Court of Appeal referred to as the 'test' for what amounts to 'comment' for the purposes of the defence. 'Comment', it said (Patrick Milmo, *Gatley on Libel and Slander,* 9th edn, 2001, Sweet & Maxwell, Chapter 12.6, and see Part Four for more details), is:

something which is or can reasonably be inferred to be a deduction, inference, conclusion, criticism, remark, observation, etc.

Examiners often take the letters to the editor scenario as the basis for a fair comment discussion. Newspapers receive numerous items of correspondence addressed to the editor for publication. The editor reserves the right to edit the letters and also to decide which ones are printed. For an example, see the House of Lords decision in *Telnikoff v. Matusevitch [1991] 4 All ER 817.* An interesting point to emerge from this case is that, when considering whether words in a letter published in a newspaper were *statements of fact* or *comment,* the court had to consider the letter in isolation. This is because there will be those who have not seen the original article or heard of the event that has been the catalyst for the correspondent to communicate with the newspaper.

The second important point to emerge from this case is that the defendant, relying on fair comment, did not have to show that the comment was an honest expression of his own views. What had to be demonstrated was that the facts on which the comment was based were true and the comment was objectively fair, in the sense that *any* person, irrespective of how prejudiced or obstinate he or she was, could honestly have held that opinion.

Overall, please note that Article 10 supports the right to express honestly held opinions. Hard-hitting satire and criticism can often be defended on the basis of honest comment. Therefore, the ability to prove absence of malice in publishing the comment becomes very significant. If malice or spite actuates a person, then it follows that he or she could not, or did not, hold the views expressed.

Privilege

This subject fits conveniently into three chunks of learning material. The first is *absolute privilege* and there is only a limited amount of information you need to know about this in order to feel confident in examinations. The second is *statutory*, or *qualified privilege*, and you will need to be aware of certain sections and schedules of the Defamation Act 1996 that cover this defence. The third, and undoubtedly the most voluminous, is *common law qualified privilege,* as expounded in *Reynolds v. Times Newspapers Ltd [2001] 2 AC 127*. This last topic is almost bound to appear in most media law examination papers or as part of your coursework because of its ongoing importance as a defence used by the media.

Absolute privilege

Become familiar with section 14 of the Defamation Act 1996. It states that a:

> fair and accurate report of proceedings in public before a court ... if published contemporaneously with the proceedings is absolutely privileged.

'A court' includes any court in the UK, the European Courts of Justice and Human Rights and international criminal tribunals established by the United Nations or by an international agreement to which the UK is a party. This reflects the principle that the courts should be open to all. Justice must be seen to be done and the media is there to provide this information to the public.

From an examination viewpoint, you need to consider the following:

- The fact that absolute privilege applies to reporting the *proceedings* only. If one reports on what happens in the public gallery and, in doing so, defames someone, then absolute privilege will not apply.
- The words *'fair,' 'accurate'* and *'contemporaneous'*. 'Fair' simply means that the reporting must be balanced in the context of informing the public what is happening in court. 'Accurate' involves reporting correctly what is said. The trainee journalist will be told to ensure accuracy when reporting names and offences with which defendants are charged. Reporting the evidence is a particular skill and you should learn to differentiate what is *alleged* from what is *fact*. 'Contemporaneous' simply means that you must publish or broadcast as soon as possible, subject to any court-imposed restrictions. Non-contemporaneous publications will presumably still attract qualified privilege because it must be in the public interest to report what is going on in court even though it may not be on the same day.

Statutory, or qualified privilege

Section 15 of the Defamation Act 1996 establishes that the publication of any report or other statement mentioned in Schedule 1 to the Act is privileged unless the publication is shown to be made with *malice*.

It is imperative that you become familiar with the provisions of Schedule 1. You will see that it is divided into two parts. Part One deals with statements having qualified privilege without explanation or contradiction. The protection is offered in seven out of the eight situations mentioned to 'fair and accurate' (but not contemporaneous) reports of the proceedings of a number of institutions or notices, advertisements or extracts from official documents. So, for example, the third item relates to a fair and accurate report of proceedings in public of a person appointed to hold a public inquiry by a government or legislature anywhere in the world. Therefore, reports of the Hutton Inquiry in 2004 attracted qualified privilege and a reporter would not have been successfully sued for defamation if, while reporting those proceedings, he or she wrote something defamatory about an individual named during the inquiry.

Part Two broadens out the categories of organisations and situations covered. They include public meetings, local authority meetings and extracts from documents circulated to members of a UK public company. Please note that the reports must be fair and accurate, but not contemporaneous.

Although we shouldn't devote much time to this, please note that the defence will be lost if the publisher of the alleged defamatory material does not provide the claimant with an opportunity to explain his or her position or contradict what has been written.

It will be seen that these schedules support the principle of freedom of speech and, in reality, amount to a public interest defence. While there have not been many instances where the courts have been troubled by these provisions, a notable exception is the House of Lords' decision in *McCarten Turkington Breen v. Times Newspapers Ltd [2001] 2 AC 277*. It was held that a press conference was a public meeting for the purposes of Schedule 1, Part Two and, therefore, the defendants could plead qualified privilege. Similar reasoning was applied to press releases, in the sense that reporters quoting from a press pack would be covered against an action if they reproduced defamatory material.

Common law qualified privilege

Of all the law associated with defences to defamation actions, this area is likely to be the most fertile for examination and coursework questions. Its popularity with the media stems from the belief that a defamation allegation should *not* succeed if the publication of it can be proved to be in the public interest. In other words, protection of reputation takes second place to freedom of expression and the public interest.

The fundamental principles of this defence were expounded in *Reynolds v. Newspapers Ltd [2001] 2 AC 127* and all students should become familiar with this case, irrespective of the type of media course being studied. The key themes to emerge (also discussed elsewhere in this book) are:

- the duty/interest test
- responsible journalism
- the ten factors – Nicholls' factors – that assist in determining whether or not the defendants have succeeded in persuading a court that its journalism was indeed 'legally' responsible (see the case notes for this case in Part Four for a description of the ten factors).

In *Jameel & Another v. Wall Street Journal Europe (No. 2) [2005] EWCA Civ 74*, the Court of Appeal considered how the test for *Reynolds* privilege should be formulated. Lord Phillips of Worth Maltravers MR offered the following (para. 87):

> the phrase responsible journalism is insufficiently precise to constitute the sole test for Reynolds privilege. It seems to us that it denotes a degree of care that a journalist should exercise before publishing a defamatory statement. The requirements of responsible journalism will vary according to the particular circumstances and, in particular, the gravity of the defamation. Responsible journalism must be demonstrated before Reynolds privilege can be estab-lished. But there is a further element that must be demonstrated. The subject matter of the publication must be of such a nature that it is in the public interest that it should be published. This is a more stringent test than that the public should be interested in receiving the information.

Any questioning relating to common law qualified privilege will usually be related to the three key themes listed above. The first is whether the defendants have established the *duty/interest test*. Newspapers, because of the vast experience of their staff, ought to know a good public interest story when one materialises. How they deal with the story will deter-mine whether or not the duty/interest test is passed. As Eady J said in the *Galloway* case, the question was whether *this* story should have been published at *that* particular time. You will need to ask, too, 'was the newspaper under a *'legal, social* or *moral'* duty to publish at that time?' You will also have to consider whether the story is in the public interest rather than the category 'of interest to the public'.

In both *Galloway [2004]* and *Armstrong [2004]*, the court found that there was *no* duty to publish at that particular time and, in the *Armstrong* case, the story itself was flawed and should not have been published then. The court, though, was prepared to accept that, if the story had been properly researched and had an adequate foundation in fact, then the public interest test would have been satisfied.

The second key theme is that of *responsible journalism*. Remember that, in *Bonnick v. Morris [2003]*, the Privy Council stated that responsible journalism is the price to be paid for the protection offered via the defence of qualified privilege.

The third key theme involves considering which of the *ten factors* are relevant in a particular case to help determine whether or not the defendant's conduct meets the criteria of what is legally responsible journalism. Not all the factors will apply. So, for example, in the *Jameel* case in 2005, the court considered the following points to be the important factors given the circumstances of this case: the seriousness of the allegation published; the nature of the information and the extent to which the subject matter was of public concern; the sources of the information; the steps taken to verify the information; the urgency to publish; confirmation sought from the claimant.

There have been various cases that have seen common law qualified privilege pleaded as the defence since the landmark *Reynolds* decision. It will be a matter of judgement, depending on the thrust of the examination question, as to which, if any, of them you cite. The ones to note, in addition to those already highlighted, are:

- *GKR Karate Ltd v. The Yorkshire Post [2000] 2 All ER 931* (see Part Four)
- *Grobbelaar v. News Group Newspapers [2001] 2 All ER 437*, where the defence lost its case because the reporting by *The Sun* amounted to a sustained character assassination that affected Grobbelaar's wife and children
- *Gaddafi v. Telegraph Group [2000] EMLR 431* (see Part Four)
- *Loutchansky v. Times Newspapers [2001] EWCA Civ 1805* (see Part Four)
- *Henry v. BBC (No. 2) [2005] EWHC 2787 (QB)* (See Part Four)
- *Roberts & Another v. Gable & Another [2006] EWHC 1025 (QB)* (see Part Four).

When embarking on the assessment of the development of common law qualified privilege, you should make reference to Lord Nicholls' expectation, expressed in *Reynolds,* that the major principles arising from the case would develop in the following few years. You should now be in a position, relying on the cases mentioned here and elsewhere, to give an authoritative account of where the law stands at the moment. The cases appear to indicate that the judiciary is quite prepared to allow the defence of common law qualified privilege to be pleaded, provided the *duty/interest test* has been passed and it is established that the comments constitute *responsible journalism*. Taking one's lead from the recent cases, this defence will be lost when newspapers publish without reasonably attempting to verify the material on which they rely. 'Should *this* material about *this* person have been published at *this* time?' is the question you must pose and attempt to answer by reference to some or all of these ten factors.

The media may claim that there are too many hurdles to jump, in the sense that they have to satisfy the majority of these factors before having a chance of success. However, this argument does not appear to have impressed the Court of Appeal in *Galloway MP v. Telegraph Group Ltd [2006] EWCA Civ 17*. In dismissing *The Daily Telegraph's* appeal, the court said (para 77) (see also Part Four):

> We see no basis upon which this court could properly interfere with the judge's conclusions ... the matters complained of were not protected by privilege because of the way in which the facts were adopted and embellished. He would have been both entitled and (in our opinion) correct to reach such a conclusion.

NB The above discussion on *Reynolds* privilege should be read in the light of the decision in *Jameel v. The Wall Street Journal Europe [2006] HL 44* (see page 174)

It will be most unusual for there to be a problem question on defamation without some reference to defences. In all probability, the defence that you will have to discuss in most detail will be common law qualified privilege, simply because of the amount of recent case law concerning this area and the fact that the principles continue to attract comment from the judiciary. Always remember that the article published must fulfil the duty/interest criteria and you must ask if this defendant was under a legal, social or moral duty to publish this article at this particular time.

2.5	
reporting restrictions	

Core Areas

- Magistrates' and Crown Courts
- Youth courts
- Adult courts
- Civil proceedings – wards of court

This topic is integral to a media law syllabus. One aspect of it is touched on in the next section when considering *postponement orders* under section 4(2) of the Contempt of Court Act 1981. This section, though, is broader, including the day-to-day restrictions faced by reporters in their endeavours to report on the courts accurately and fairly for the benefit of the public.

The first question you are likely to have to ponder is whether or not the principles justifying reporting restrictions are consistent with the media's rights to freedom of expression and open justice?

The answer is to be found in the interplay between Articles 10 and 6. Everyone has the right to express their views freely, but, equally, everyone has a right to a fair trial. Therefore, occasionally, there will be a need to impose restrictions on the reporting of what occurs in the courts and prior to a trial. This latter point is examined in the next section on the Contempt of Court Act. Our focus here will be on the trial process itself. This section will probably be of more interest to trainee journalists as opposed to those on undergraduate courses. Nevertheless, the latter should not ignore this topic as it frequently appears on undergraduate examination papers.

The first, and perhaps most basic, point is that you should become reasonably familiar with the major elements of the criminal and civil justice systems. It is unrealistic for you to be expected to know the ins and outs of the procedures relevant to each system, but a basic working knowledge can only help your cause. To this end, the hierarchy of the courts needs to be understood.

Magistrates' and Crown Courts

Trainee journalists will invariably spend much of their early years reporting from magistrates' and Crown Courts, so a familiarity with what types of crimes are dealt with at each level will help to prevent mistakes being made. Magistrates, in the main, deal with low-level crimes – referred to as *summary* offences. Most serious crimes – known as *indictable* offences, are tried in the Crown Court before a jury. Juries do not hear cases in magistrates' courts. Some apparently serious offences can be tried in either the Crown Court or magistrates' court. However, for example, a theft of a small sum of money would rarely if ever result in a defendant being tried for the offence at Crown Court.

Youth courts

When magistrates are sitting to hear a case against a person under the age of 18, then they are constituted as a youth court. The crucial point to remember here is that anonymity is granted to the defendant and a report or broadcast should not include information from which that person's identity could be ascertained. This restriction is contained in section 49 of the Children and Young Person's Act 1933. However, anonymity can be lifted in three circumstances:

- to avoid injustice to the juvenile
- when the public interest requires that anonymity to be lifted
- if the authorities need to trace a juvenile in connection with a serious offence (section 49(4A)).

The topic that is most likely to attract your examiner's attention is the second one because it begs the question, 'In what circumstances does the public interest demand that anonymity be lifted?'

An important case to mention when addressing this matter is *T. v. Director of Public Prosecutions & North East Press [2003] EWHC 2408*. You will need to read this case together with the important decision in *McKerry v. Teesdale & Wear Valley Justices [2000] Crim LR 594*. In the latter case, the Divisional Court held that the power to dispense with anonymity had to be exercised with great care. It should not be done for reasons of naming and shaming or as an additional punishment. The court thought that it would *rarely* be deemed to be in the public interest for anonymity to be withdrawn. The court, in coming to its decision, could also invite any reporters present to offer their opinions. The magistrates will find themselves in a position of having to balance the young person's right to anonymity against the need to demonstrate that justice is administered in public and there is open and fair reporting of the proceedings. In other words, they must take into account the relevant European jurisprudence relating to Articles 10 and 8.

In the former case, Sullivan J thought that the purpose of the anonymity rule was to protect young persons 'from the adverse consequences of publicity.' The importance of this case, however, is it established that the anonymity provisions will not apply once the defendant has reached the age of 18. In this case, the defendant turned 18 while the youth court was still dealing with the case. It was held that the press could report the full facts, including identity, as section 49 no longer applied in these circumstances.

Another likely subject for examination questions involving the youth court involves assessing antisocial behaviour legislation and its interplay with the youth court anonymity provisions.

In brief, the current situation is that if an application for an Antisocial Behaviour Order (ASBO) is made after a young person has been convicted in a youth court, then the press are under two different reporting regimes. In a youth court, they are barred from identifying the defendant under section 49. However, when dealing with an application for an ASBO, the magistrates are sitting in a *civil*, not *criminal*, capacity and so it is possible to report on identity. The difficulty though, is that in reporting the ASBO, no mention should be made of the youth court proceedings, otherwise that reporting will lead the newspaper to breach section 49. To further complicate matters, if the ASBO is then breached, the matter will be dealt with in a youth court. Until recently, this meant that the press could not identify the young person who had breached the ASBO because of the section 49 anonymity provisions.

I say 'until recently' because the government has responded to representations by the press that the restriction makes adequate reporting almost impossible. As a result of section 141 of the Serious Organised Crime and Police Act 2005, section 49 will not apply, no longer preventing the reporting of the identity of a young person who has breached an ASBO. Instead, the magistrates will have the power to dispense with anonymity under powers granted by section 45 of the Youth Justice and Criminal Evidence Act 1999. If the magistrates do decide to exercise the power to permit the press to identify the miscreant, however, then reasons will have to be given (see section 141(2) of the 2005 Act).

Adult courts

The opposite presumption regarding the anonymity of adults and juveniles applies in magistrates' and Crown Courts. In other words, there is no *automatic* presumption of anonymity. You must mention the House of Lords decision in *Re. S (FC) (a child) (Appellant) [2004] UKHL 47*, to the effect that departure from the open justice principle is 'exceptional'. Examiners are likely to explore this area of law from the following perspectives.

Juveniles

Where a juvenile is charged with a serious offence, such as murder, and appears at the Crown Court, there is no automatic presumption that the press should not identify the defendant. However, section 39 of the Children and Young Persons Act 1933 bestows discretion on the judge to ban reporting.

On what basis might a judge decide to exercise discretion in favour of the defendant? What might constitute good reasons? It is reasonable to assume that judges are keen to protect young people from having their identity revealed, but that must be balanced against the seriousness of the case and the needs of open justice. You may wish to mention that, at the Jamie Bulger trial, the defendants, Thompson and Venables, were not named, but the judge did lift the section 39 order *after* conviction.

One approach is to look at the issue on a case-by-case basis. Age and the likely *impact* of identification will be important factors (see *R. v. Lee [1993] 2 All ER 170*) It will also help your understanding of the issue if you consider the decision of Simon Brown LJ in *R. v. Winchester Crown Court ex parte B [2000] 1 Cr App Rep 11,* in which a number of principles were identified that a judge should take into account when considering whether or not to make a section 39 order:

- Are there good reasons for naming the defendant?
- The court must take into account the welfare of the young person.
- Will naming the defendant send out a message that will act as deterrent to others?
- What is the defendant's age and what is the likely impact of publication upon him?
- Judges should balance the demand to name in support of the principle of open justice against the likely impact on the defendant of naming him.

Also, in November 2005, at Oxford Crown Court, a father and his two sons were found guilty of murder in the so-called 'Honour killings' case.

The youngest son was 16 and, at the beginning of the trial, the judge imposed a section 39 order. After conviction, the media requested that the order be lifted. Gross J acceded to the request because of the seriousness of the offence. He rejected submissions by prosecution counsel that the defendant was an exceptionally vulnerable young man who had not fully appreciated the gravity of the offence for which he had been found guilty.

You must also be aware that the Press Complaints Commission's Code of Practice (clause 7) bans the reporting of the names of children under 16 who are *victims* or *witnesses* in cases involving sex offences.

The issue of whether or not to impose reporting restrictions in the case of child participants in criminal proceedings was fully considered by the House of Lords in the *Re. S (FC) (a Child)* case in 2004.

Adults

One trap that may be set is if the examiner asks you to determine if an adult defendant should not be named in order to protect children in the family. In *Re. S (FC) (a child) [2004]* the mother was found guilty of unlawfully killing her son. The House of Lords allowed the press to name her at her trial even though she had another young son who was not a party to the proceedings and who, it was argued, would be adversely affected by the publicity should the mother be named (see Part Four for further details).

When it comes to cases where the defendant has been charged with a sexual offence, there is no provision for anonymity, which is in complete contrast to the *victim* of an alleged sexual offence. This may well be an issue that you are expected to debate in a tutorial – why the defendant is not granted anonymity but the victim is? A straw poll among my students suggested that they would be overwhelmingly in favour of granting anonymity to both the victim *and* defendant in cases of serious sexual offences. The overriding reason seemed to be that, even though the defendant might be acquitted, there will still be those who would be convinced that he committed the crime.

The law has changed. The Sexual Offences Act 2003 increased the number of offences for which a complainant is entitled to anonymity. The Act came into force in May 2004. Also, on 7 October 2004, section 48 and parts of Schedule 2 of the Youth Justice and Criminal Evidence Act 1999 came into force, with the effect that the protection offered by the Sexual Offences (Amendment) Act 1992 has been *extended* in favour of the complainant. The anonymity protection offered now commences once an *allegation* of a sexual offence has been made. Nothing must be published that is likely to lead members of the public to identifying the complainant during that person's lifetime. A similar provision applied, and continues to apply, after a person has been *accused* of a sexual offence.

You should also note that the amended 1992 Act, for the first time, includes examples of what *cannot* be used in reporting the story. Obvious examples include name, address and occupation, but it is made clear to both newspapers and broadcasters that 'no still or moving image of the person may be used' (section 3A).

In February 2006 *The Daily Telegraph* and *Daily Express* were fined for breaches of the Sexual Offences (Amendment) Act 1992 when they published photographs of the victim of an alleged sexual assault. The photograph showed a rear view of the victim. The newspapers had been covering a court martial and the alleged victim, a member of the armed forces, was photographed while she was wearing her uniform. Arguably this would make identification easier in the particular community in which she resided than if she had been in everyday clothes. Another newspaper was not prosecuted for using the same photograph because it had manipulated the image.

While we are dealing with recent changes to the law in this area, please note the bringing into force in October 2004 of section 46 of the Youth Justice and Criminal Evidence Act 1999. This section has implemented the 'vulnerable witness' provisions and, consequently, there are implications for the media in terms of reporting restrictions. While the idea of protecting the identities of vulnerable witnesses on whom the outcome of a trial may depend is laudable, in deciding whether or not to make such an order, the court must consider if, from the media's point of view, the interests of justice are being served.

Of current interest is the use of 'lifetime' injunctions to prevent reporting on the whereabouts and identity of high-profile defendants once they have been released from prison. Such an injunction was granted to Maxine Carr on 24 February 2005. The injunction, contra mundum, that had already been granted the previous year was continued indefinitely. Eady J accepted that the only way to protect her rights under Article 2 of the ECHR was to grant the injunction. In doing so, he made legal history – granting such an extensive injunction to a person who had not been convicted of a serious offence. It will be recalled she had been convicted of perverting the course of justice in providing an alibi for Ian Huntley, the Soham murderer. See also the decisions of Dame Elizabeth Butler-Sloss, the President of the Family Division of the High Court, in granting similar injunctions to Mary Bell and Robert

Thompson and Jon Venables (*[2003] EWHC 1101 (QB)* and *[2001] EWHC QB 32*

Civil proceedings – wards of court

Questions on this area of the law invariably centre on children and whether or not the media may report their identities. In Children Act 1989 proceedings, anonymity for persons under 18 applies in the High Court and county court as well as family proceedings in a magistrates' court.

The topic most likely to be under consideration in this context is the wardship jurisdiction. Children may be made wards of court either by their parents or as a result of the intervention of local authorities acting in the interests of the child. Difficulties often ensue when a teenage child goes against the wishes of his or her parents and, as a result, the parents turn to the court for assistance.

Your first port of call should be section 12 of the Administration of Justice Act 1960. You need to be careful with the interpretation of this section. Designed to limit reporting in *private* proceedings, it will only be a contempt if *information* about the *proceedings* in question is published. Therefore, simply to state that wardship proceedings are being heard will not be contempt. In *BBC v. Kelly [2001] Fam 59*, Munby J decided that the media could interview a ward of court and publish or broadcast such an interview without the permission of the court. This was subject to the proviso that there was no breach of section 12 of the Administration of Justice Act 1960, nor section 97(2) of the Children Act, as amended by the Access to Justice Act 1999, otherwise it would be contempt. In practice, this usually means that the story can be told, but the ward cannot be named, nor any mention made of the details of any proceedings held in private.

Alternatively, there would appear to be no embargo on writing about a ward and identifying him or her, providing it is not mentioned that he or she is a ward or reference made to private proceedings.

The law has been further complicated by the fact that there have been numerous authorities relating to publicity in wardship proceedings that, arguably, have created a recipe for confusion. As Munby J said in *Torbay Borough Council v. News Group Newspapers [2003] EWHC 2927 (Fam)* (para. 14) 'As is notorious this is a branch of law where there has been much judicial activity over the last 25 years.'

I will list the most important cases for reasons that will become obvious a little later. They are:

- *In re. X. (A Minor) [1975] Fam 47*
- *In re. C. (A Minor) [1990] Fam 39*
- *In re. M. & N. (Minors) [1990] Fam 211*
- *In re. W. (A Minor) [1992] 1 WLR 100*
- *In re. H. (Minor) [1994] 1 FLR 519*
- *R. v. Central Independent Television PLC [1994] Fam 192*
- *In re. R. (Wardship) [1994] Fam 254*
- *In re. Z. (A Minor) [1997] Fam 1.*

Prior to the Human Rights Act coming into force, it was generally accepted that there were three elements to the wardship, or 'inherent', jurisdiction. In the first category, the jurisdiction was not exercisable at all usually when the child was to be treated in the same way as an adult and therefore the jurisdiction was inappropriate. Second, the jurisdiction was appropriate because the court was exercising its *protective* function regarding the child. Here, the child's interests were not paramount. Third, the court was exercising a custodial jurisdiction where the child's interests were paramount. It will be clear that the courts in categories two and three were carrying out a balancing exercise between the right of the press to report and the need to protect the child's identity.

However, as the judge said in the *Torbay* case, the above analysis 'had to be revisited in the light of the Human Rights Act 1998.' The analysis has now been undertaken by the House of Lords in *Re. S (FC) (a child) [2004]* and, as a consequence, the list of authorities above was 'downgraded' with the words:

> That is not to say that the case law on the inherent jurisdiction of the High court is wholly irrelevant. On the contrary, it may remain of some interest in regard to the ultimate balancing exercise to be carried out under the ECHR provisions.

Hardly a ringing endorsement, I'm sure you'll agree. The approach to be adopted now must conform to the 'new methodology required by the ECHR as explained in *Campbell v. MGN Ltdl'* (per Lord Steyn, para. 23).

The long and short of it is that, as the house said, the 'ultimate balancing exercise' must now be carried out under the ECHR provisions. In other words, the issue will be seen as a contest between the right to privacy under Article 8 and the right to free expression under Article 10.

In conclusion, it must be noted that the House was dealing with the identity issue in criminal proceedings, but the reference to 'inherent jurisdiction' would suggest that, subject to section 12 of the 1960 Act and section 97(2) of the Children Act 1989, the determination of a dispute regarding identifying a person under 18 who is a ward of court is still likely to be made by balancing Article 8 with Article 10. As in the *Torbay* case, the two Articles may, in fact, be complimentary. The court there decided that the young person, then aged 17, who wished to tell her story via the press, should be permitted to do so. You should also look at the case *In the Matter of B (A Child) [2004] EWHC 411*. In it, the judge concluded that it might be considered counterproductive to overzealously attempt to keep family court proceedings private.

Public confidence in the family court system could be enhanced if more matters were permitted to enter into the public domain. This is a current issue so do some research (see, for example, in the 'Articles' section of the www.5rb.co.uk website under the heading 'Reporting the Courts, Adam Wolanski's article entitled 'Children, experts and open justice in the Family Division', 13 March 2006).

The same kind of more open approach was also taken in invoking the inherent jurisdiction in the case of a mentally impaired adult in the case of *E. v. Channel 4 Television & Another [2005] EWHC 1144 (Fam)*.

The question that remains to be answered in the future is, 'In what circumstances is Article 8 likely to prevail over Article 10?' For the moment, Article 10 appears to hold the upper hand. The developments occurring in the law on privacy will obviously have an impact on this aspect of the law. It is an area that promises to develop over the coming years and so should loom large in examination questions.

2.6	
contempt of court	

Core Areas

- Purpose of the contempt laws as they relate to trials
- The key words
- Can there be contempt *and* a safe conviction?
- What conduct will actually be found to be contempt?
- Fair and accurate reports
- Discussion of public affairs

Like defamation, this topic is almost certain to appear in most examination papers. There are several elements to the law relating to contempt of court, the major ones being:

- contravention of the strict liability provisions in section 2 of the Contempt of Court Act 1981
- the imposition of postponement orders under section 4(2) of the 1981 Act
- protection of sources under section 10 of the 1981 Act
- protection of juries from media intrusion under section 8 of the 1981 Act
- the difference between common law and statutory contempt.

Purpose of the contempt laws as they relate to trials

The primary purpose of the law is to ensure that a fair trial can be achieved, as required by Article 6 of the European Convention on Human Rights. The presumption is that this objective is more likely to be attained if the press do not engage in potentially prejudicial reporting either prior to or during the course of a trial than if this was not the case.

The starting point for your analysis must be the provisions of section 2 of the 1981 Act:

> The strict liability rule applies only to a publication that creates a substantial risk that the course of justice in the proceedings in question will be seriously impeded or prejudiced.

The reference to 'strict liability' in section 2 of the Act means that liability may ensue even though the publisher of the information has no *intention* to interfere with 'the course of justice in particular legal proceedings.'

The critical point for you to remember is that the provisions of the Act do not apply until proceedings have become 'active' within the terms of section 2(3) of the Act. For example, a warrant has been issued for a suspect's arrest or he or she has been arrested. This is the 'initial step' required for reporters to be put on notice that consideration should be given to the purpose of the legislation.

The Attorney General often reminds newspaper editors and broadcasting organisations of their responsibilities under the Act (as if they need reminding!). By way of example, the following advisory was issued to the media by the Attorney General's Office on 18 January 2005 at the commencement of the trial of British soldiers for allegedly abusing Iraqi detainees:

> The Attorney [General] reminds editors of their obligations not to engage in conduct, nor publish material, including comment, that might create a substantial risk of serious prejudice to the course of justice in the proceedings ... [He] particularly urges all newspapers, broadcasters and other parties to take note of the risks in publishing material that asserts or assumes, expressly or implicitly, the guilt of the accused persons.

An important point to emphasise to your examiners is that the Act is used sparingly, in the sense that few cases come before the High Court. Section 7 of the Contempt of Court Act 1981 provides that possible contempt proceedings must be referred to the Attorney General, who will decide whether or not to bring an action. Many are referred; few make it all the way!

I might be so bold as to suggest two major themes for your consideration, based on the likely approach of examiners. The first is the 'black letter' analysis – that is, of the words – of Section 2 of the Act. Students studying for a Bachelor of Laws (LLB) degree may expect this type of question. The second is more practical and involves looking at the question, 'In light of the reporting prior to and during the trial of Ian Huntley for the Soham murders in October 2003, do the relevant provisions of the 1981 Act need to be reviewed and updated?'

The key words

'Substantial risk'

The risk must be *practical* rather than *theoretical* or *illusory*. This was determined by the Queen's Bench Divisional Court in *Attorney General v. Guardian Newspapers Ltd & Another [1992] 3 All ER 38*, per Mann LJ. The critical question, he said, (at p.45 (b)) was not whether or not the published material was of a type:

> which is inherently likely to create the requisite risk ... the crucial question is ... whether ... the publication created at the time of its publication a substantial risk that the course of justice would be seriously impeded or prejudiced. The risk must be a practical risk and not a theoretical risk.

Kerr J said, (para 12) *In the matter of an application by Her Majesty's Attorney General for Northern Ireland [2003] NIQB 73*, that, 'All but trivial risk is covered by section 2 (2)'.

The Court in *Attorney General v. Express Newspapers [2004] EWHC 2859 (Admin)* (para 5) summed up the matter in the following way:

'Substantial risk' in section 2(2) means a risk which is more than remote (Attorney General v. English [1983] 1AC 116 at pages141H to 142 C per Lord Diplock) or 'not insubstantial' (Attorney General v. News Group [1987] QB1 at 15C per John Donaldson MR) or as Mr Caldecott (counsel) prefers to express it 'real'. The risk must be practical and not theoretical.

In that short paragraph, you have the most recent authoritative statement on the meaning of substantial risk. Read and digest!

'Serious'

Whether the risk is *serious* or not will depend on a number of factors. The *timing* of the publication is important. If the material is published two days before a trial is to begin, then there will be an assumption that potential jury members will see the material and may well be influenced by it.

The second important matter will be the *content* of the material. An obvious example is where the article assumes guilt or previous convictions are published. In such circumstances, serious prejudice may be more readily inferred than if these matters are not included. (Although, now note the 'bad character' provisions contained in sections 98 and 99 of the Criminal Justice Act 2003, which came into force in December 2004. This permits evidence of previous bad character, including convictions, to be drawn to the court's attention should they tend to denote a 'pattern' of behaviour relevant to the proceedings before the court.)

One should also ponder whether or not the material would have been likely to have come to the attention of potential jurors and, if it had, if it would be likely to remain in their memories. This allows the court to consider the 'fade factor'. This was so important in persuading the judge in the *Huntley and Carr* case that the lapse of time between potentially prejudicial material being published and the trial was sufficient that jury members, properly directed, would not be influenced by what they had seen in the newspapers and on television months before. The judge had, on the 9 June, issued a postponement order that, in effect, amounted to a total embargo on reporting between that date and the commencement of the trial.

For the avoidance of any doubt, at 16.30 on 9th June 2003 Mr Justice Moses made an order under section 4(2) of the Contempt of Court Act 1981 prohibiting publication of any report revealing or tending to reveal the detail of the evidence against Ian Kevin Huntley and/or any other material relating to or about him until such time as proceedings against him and/or his co-defendant Maxine Carr are concluded. (Attorney General's Legal Advisory, June 2003)

What is clear is that what is right for each case will depend on its own set of facts and circumstances. So, for example, if the publication in which the 'offending' material is published circulates only in the North East of England and the trial is to take place at Southampton Crown Court, then it most unlikely to have any impact at all on potential jury members.

It will be apparent that, while we are considering two separate sets of words, they do, in practice, overlap to a certain degree. As proof of legal recognition of that fact, see Auld LJ in *Attorney General v. BBC [1997] EMLR 76*, p. 81.

The court has to be convinced, beyond all reasonable doubt, that there has been a substantial risk of serious prejudice. You will be obliged to refer to the case law mentioned above, but, eventually, you will have to point out that a judgment needs to be reached on the *particular* facts and circumstances of the case set before you.

Can there be contempt and a safe conviction?

Authority would suggest that the answer to this question is 'Yes'. This might happen when a trial has 'been moved or delayed to minimise the prejudice occasioned by some publication' (Simon Brown LJ in *Attorney General v. Unger & Others [1998] 1 Cr App R 309*, pp. 318–9).

The assumption is that section 2(2) (Simon Brown LJ in *Attorney General v. Birmingham Post & Mail [1999] 1 WLR 361*, p. 369H):

> postulates a lesser degree of prejudice than is required to make good an appeal against conviction [or] ... justify an order for a stay. In short s.2(2) is designed to avoid (and where necessary punish) publications even if they merely risk prejudicing proceedings, whereas a stay will generally only be granted where it is recognised that any subsequent conviction would otherwise be imperilled, and a conviction will only be set aside if it is actually unsafe.

However, a different view was expressed by Collins J in *Attorney General v. Guardian Newspapers Ltd [1999] All ER (D), p. 856*. In his opinion, the prejudice required by section 2(2), which must be serious, was not of a lesser degree 'than that required to make good an appeal against conviction.' The prejudice must, he thought, be sufficient to constitute a stay or appeal against conviction. His plea was for uniformity of approach. In the same case, Sedley LJ opined that the courts 'should not speak with a robust voice in criminal appeals and a sensitive one in contempt cases.' He thought that there should be a 'single standard' and it should be recognised that 'it will operate differently in the two contexts.' The judge emphasised that, in contempt cases, the risk had to be gauged prospectively – and, therefore, without regard to the outcome of the trial – but, in a criminal appeal, this had to be done retrospectively.

He went on to say that one way to ensure consistency of approach was to test the accusation of contempt by assuming that:

- jurors *had* read the publication
- an application to discharge the jury had been made and refused
- the judge had given the jury proper direction to disregard anything that they had read
- a conviction was not inevitable
- the jury have convicted.

Having done all that, if an appeal against conviction based on prejudice would not succeed, the publisher should not be guilty of contempt.

This approach can be applied only when the case has gone to trial. It would not be helpful in a situation such as the one that arose in *Attorney General v. Express Newspapers Ltd [2004] EWHC 2859 (Admin)*. Here, the Crown Prosecution Service decided not to bring criminal charges against footballers named by the *Daily Star*. Nevertheless, the *Daily Star's* conduct in naming the players despite police appeals to the contrary was held to be contempt and the newspaper was fined £60,000 plus costs.

What conduct will actually be found to be contempt?

In summing up a problem question, you will inevitably have to decide, on the facts and the law that you have considered, whether or not the media organisation has created a *substantial* risk of *serious* prejudice. It has been stated above that this may be difficult to determine as everything will depend on the circumstances. It is reasonable to assume that judges will not wish to stay proceedings, so, if they can be postponed or moved, then perhaps no contempt proceedings will be brought. However, that does not automatically follow. In the *Belfast Sunday Life* case, the trial was delayed in order for the fade factor to kick in. Nevertheless, the paper was fined £4,000 and the editor £1,000.

You would be well advised to identify a small number of cases to use by way of illustration. Here are three examples. In *Attorney General v. BBC & Hat Trick Productions [1997] EMLR 76,* the popular BBC programme *Have I Got News For You* referred to the sons of Robert Maxwell as 'heartless scheming bastards.' This was transmitted some six months before the date fixed for their trial on fraud charges. The respondents were, nevertheless, found guilty of contempt. The judge viewed that these words were 'strikingly prejudicial and go to the heart of the case' (fraud). (He went on (Quoted in *Attorney General v. Birmingham Post and Mail Ltd [1998] EWHC 769 (Admin) para 31*):

> I am sure that the broadcast created such a risk, namely that one or more jurors would not begin and continue their jury duty with an open mind, and thus that there was a substantial risk that the course of justice in the trial would be seriously prejudiced.

In *Attorney General v. Unger, Manchester Evening News and Associated Newspapers [1997] EWHC 624 (Admin),* reporters interviewed a woman caught on videotape apparently stealing money from an old lady. She 'confessed' to the reporters after being shown the tape. Subsequently, the *Manchester Evening News* and the *Daily Mail* published the story, together with her 'confession' and included clips from the videotape. The newspapers had sought legal advice, which was to the effect that, despite proceedings being *active,* there was little chance of contempt because of the confession and the videotape evidence. In other words, no jury could possibly be influenced by newspaper reports if shown the tapes and confession.

The court restated the principle that, in this country, we do not welcome trial by media. The Divisional Court reminded editors that simply because someone has 'confessed' does not mean that they will plead 'guilty'. (The *Grobbelaar* prosecution comes to mind, in which he was acquitted despite being shown on camera apparently discussing and receiving money to throw football matches.)

Nevertheless, the newspapers were acquitted of contempt because of the fade factor. Jurors' memories, apparently, are not as good as those of the rest of the population!

A good case to familiarise yourself with is *Attorney General v. ITN & Others [1995] 2 All ER 370.* This case covers actions by both television news programmes and newspapers concerning the arrest of two men subsequently charged with murder. It was reported that one of the men was a convicted IRA terrorist who had escaped from jail in Belfast. A poor photograph of him was also shown on television. However, later bulletins omitted this information. Four newspapers published details in their first editions only about his alleged terrorist links, but only one omitted the fact that he had been convicted of murdering an SAS officer.

The court held that contempt had not been proved. The 'offending' broadcast was deemed to have been 'brief and ephemeral in nature.' The circulation of the first editions of the newspapers in the London area amounted, in total, to approximately 5,000. Therefore, because of the relatively small circulation and the passing of time between publication and trial, the Attorney General was held not to have proved his case.

Fair and accurate reports

Do note the provisions of section 4 of the Contempt of Court Act 1981. A person is not guilty of contempt under the strict liability rule if he or she produces a *fair and accurate report* of *legal proceedings* held in *public* and publishes it *contemporaneously* and in *good faith*. This provision has echoes of the protection offered by the Defamation Act 1996 (sections 14 and 15) to reporters who might accidentally defame someone while reporting on the courts.

You should remember that the protection offered here is conditional on a report relating to the *proceedings* and nothing else said or done in court. It must be assumed that any publication by a responsible newspaper *will* be in good faith. 'Contemporaneous' simply means as soon as practically possible after the event.

Of more interest perhaps to examiners will be the use of postponement orders under section 4(2) of the Act. If a court believes that there will be a substantial risk of prejudice if a report of the proceedings, or *any other proceedings,* is published, then a postponement order may be made. That will usually be for a limited period of time, although it has been known for a postponement order to run for nearly four years. In October 2004, the Press Association reported on the case of a solicitor convicted of conspiracy to defraud at Bristol Crown Court in January 2001. Details of the case were only allowed to be published in 2004, after the case against the last of 21 former employees also facing charges was allowed to lie on the file.

Section 4(2) orders should not be confused with section 11 orders. The key word in section 4(2) is *postponement.* Section 11 permits a court to order that a person's name should not be published once the judge has ruled that the person, usually a witness, should have his or her name withheld from the public. This is a 'limited use' provision which will normally be invoked where national security considerations are involved, such as when a member of the security services has been called to give evidence, but, for obvious reasons, does not wish to have his or her identity exposed. Another possible use of section 11 orders would be to prevent blackmail victims from being named in court. This assists the administration of justice because it is likely to encourage blackmail victims to be more prepared to bring the crime to the attention of the authorities.

Discussion of public affairs

The preparation for an important trial can take many months. The trial itself may also take many months. With the Contempt of Court Act being operative from the moment proceedings become active, it could be argued that this represents an unnecessary restriction on the right to free expression. Section 5 was included in an attempt to address the imbalance.

In *Attorney General v. Times Newspapers Ltd [1973] 3 All ER 54 (HL)*, the newspaper had intended to bring to the attention of the public information about how the drug thalidomide had been marketed. This drug had been taken by pregnant women and there was a link established between the drug and a number of women who gave birth to children with deformities. The House of Lords held that, as there were a number of civil actions pending against the Distillers company, the public interest lay in 'protecting' the administration of justice rather than public discussion of the issues raised. (*The Sunday Times* eventually took the issue to the European Court of Justice and won a ruling that the decision had violated Article 10 of the European Convention on Human Rights.)

This topic frequently appears on examination papers. The key case to familiarise yourself with is *Attorney General v. English [1983] 1 AC 116 [1982] 2 All ER 903 at p. 198(g)*. The importance of section 5 was explained by Lord Diplock thus (see Part Four for brief details of this case):

> Section 5 does not take the form of a proviso or an exception to s.2(2). It stands on an equal footing with it ... it states what publications shall not amount to contempt of court despite their tendency to interfere with the course of justice in particular legal proceedings.

Juries

Juries are accorded special mention in the Contempt of Court Act (see section 8). It is contempt to:

> obtain, disclose or solicit any particular statements made, opinions expressed, arguments advanced or votes cast by members of a jury in the course of their deliberations in any legal proceedings.

From a media law perspective, the jury, when acting in its appointed role, is sacrosanct.

This 'ring of steel' protection accorded to the jury is currently the subject of investigation because it appears to be at odds with Article 6 of the European Convention on Human Rights. You will recall that this Article confirms the right of every individual to a fair trial. The question is, 'How can this be guaranteed if one is unaware of what takes place in the jury room?'

The House of Lords in *Regina v. Connor and Mizra [2004] UKHL 2*, confirmed that, after a trial had concluded, any doubts expressed to the judge by a juror could not form the basis of an appeal against conviction unless the actions of the jurors undermined the true function of the jury – for example, by deciding guilt as a result of tossing a coin.

In January 2005, the Department for Constitutional Affairs published a consultation paper, the aim of which is to discover what more can be done to help jurors perform their role and improve their overall experience as jurors. One major question is, 'What happens if there are allegations of improper behaviour in the jury room, to the extent that a fair trial is threatened?'

The current position was initially determined by the House of Lords in the case of *Attorney General v. Associated Newspapers [1994] 1 ALL ER 556*. Stated simply, the position is that disclosure of the deliberations of a jury amounts to contempt. That is the case even if the information is obtained 'indirectly'. The proper administration of justice requires that jury discussions are unfettered and uninhibited (see Part Four for more details of this case.)

> *The Contempt of Court Act 1981 is fertile ground for examination questions. Invariably the focus will be on the strict liability rule and in particular the interpretation of the section 2(2) criteria. Questions relating to the relationship between juries and the media will also be prevalent because of the current issues surrounding the Article 6 'dilemma' of being able to prove that a fair trial has taken place. Therefore become familiar with the terms of section 8 of the 1981 Act.*

2.7

protection of sources

Core Areas

- Section 10
- Development of law by study of cases
- Other legislative considerations

Although this subject matter is covered by the Contempt of Court Act 1981, the protection of sources topic is often treated as a discrete entity by examiners, so this is the approach that I shall adopt here.

The starting point is section 10 of the 1981 Act. This section appears to give support to a fundamental principle of journalism, that reporters are under a professional duty to protect their sources of information. The assumption is that the free flow of information will be reduced to a trickle if journalists cannot give anonymity to the sources of stories. The 'responsible journalism' principle examined above assumes a degree of correlation between the credibility of the source and the protection offered by common law qualified privilege. In the context of contempt of court, the protection offered to journalists is strong, but 'qualified'.

The first thing you must do is become familiar with the words of section 10:

> No court may require a person to disclose, nor is any person guilty of contempt of court for refusing to disclose, the source of information contained in a publication for which he is responsible, unless it is established to the satisfaction of the court that disclosure is necessary in the interests of justice or national security or for the prevention of disorder or crime.

It will be immediately apparent that there are several key words or phrases here that will attract your examiner's attention. These are:

- 'necessary'
- 'interests of justice'
- 'national security'
- 'prevention of disorder or crime'.

Taking the above into account, the following are the links you need to pursue in order to demonstrate an understanding of these issues.

A good starting point is the definitive speech of Lord Bridge in the leading case of *X Limited v. Morgan Grampian (Publishers) Limited [1991] AC 1* and the subsequent decision of the European Court of Human Rights in *Goodwin v. United Kingdom (1996) 22EHRR 123*. An important statement of principle was given in the latter case (p. 143):

> Protection of journalistic sources is one of the basic conditions for press free-
> dom ... without such protection, sources may be deterred from assisting the
> press in informing the public on matters of public interest. As a result the vital
> public watchdog role of the press may be undermined and the ability of the
> press to provide accurate and reliable information may be adversely affected.

This principle should underpin your investigation of the law in this area. However, you would do well to consider two things. First, why was it necessary to include section 10 in the Contempt of Court Act and, second, since coming into force, what has been the approach of the judiciary to its interpretation?

The answer to the first question is to be found in the decision of the House of Lords in *British Steel Corporation v. Granada Television [1981] 1 All ER 417*. In this case, Granada had used a substantial number of documents that it had received unsolicited from a source within British Steel, the workforce of which, at the time, was subject to a national strike. The programme highlighted mismanagement within British Steel. Granada promised the informant that his identity would remain confidential. British Steel sought an order for Granada to disclose the identity of its source based on two grounds:

- to prevent further misuse of British Steel documents
- to remove suspicion from those staff who had access to such documents as the ones revealed to Granada.

The House of Lords, by a 4:1 majority, ordered Granada to reveal the identity of the source. The House accepted that British Steel had suffered a wrong and was being denied the right to remedy the wrong because it didn't know the identity of the person who had breached confidentiality. The overriding principle seemed to be that the public interest in doing justice outweighed any public interest in its being informed about the steel strike. However, in a strong dissenting speech, Lord Salmon emphasised that protection of sources *was* in the public interest and, in the past, only where national security was at stake would that immunity be lifted. It was

Lord Salmon's view that carried the day when Parliament passed the Contempt of Court Act.

The second question involves the analysis of a significant number of cases. Space does not permit me to go into great detail here, but you need to consider the following cases, noting the contribution each makes to the development of the law.

The first major decision after the Act came into force did not bode well for a liberal interpretation of section 10. In *Secretary of State for Defence v. Guardian Newspapers [1984] 3 All ER 601,* the House of Lords, by a 3:2 majority, held that the Crown had, on the balance of probabilities, established the 'national security' exception. The point to press home is that the majority placed a very 'narrow' interpretation on the words 'interests of justice'. This term was deemed to refer to the:

> *administration of justice in the course of legal proceedings in a court of law, a tribunal or a body exercising the judicial power of the state and not the concept of justice in the abstract. (at p. 602(d))*

As you might expect, a disappointing outcome for the media. A year later, the House considered the meaning of 'necessary' within section 10 and came to the conclusion (see: *Re. an inquiry under the Company Securities (Insider Dealing) Act 1985 [1988] 1 All ER 203*, per Lord Griffiths, p. 208–9) that it:

> *has a meaning that lies somewhere between 'indispensable' on the one hand and 'useful' or 'expedient' on the other and leave it to the judge to decide towards which end of the scale of meaning he will place it on the facts of any particular case. The nearest paraphrase I can suggest is 'really needed'.*

From here, you can move on to the vitally important duo of cases that constitute the legal proceedings associated with William Goodwin, a trainee journalist (see Part Four for further details). This case is notable for the departure from the 'narrow' meaning given to the term 'interests of justice' in the *Guardian* case of 1984. The view taken in the above case by Lord Bridge of Harwich was that a wider interpretation was appropriate – that the term meant 'interests that are justiciable' rather than 'the administration of justice in the course of legal proceedings in a court of law' as we saw above.

It is vital that, once you have read this case, you progress to the European Court of Human Rights' decision in *Goodwin v. United Kingdom [1996] 22 EHRR 123*. Having failed to convince the House of Lords of the merits of his case, Goodwin took the government to court on the basis that section 10 was incompatible with his rights under Article 10 of the Convention. He won the case. However, in the next case, the Court of Appeal took the view that the English and European courts were not at odds on the importance to be attached to Article 10. The difference lay in the conclusions based on the facts rather than in any fundamental difference in *approach* to its interpretation.

The final stage in this analysis of the case law for this topic is to look at the post-2000 cases. The issue of section 10 protection has arisen in a number of cases since the onset of the new millennium. In *John & Others v. Express Newspapers [2000] EWCA Civ 135,* counsel's opinion had been sought on financial matters relating to Sir Elton John. The advice was sent to his solicitors and a draft copy ripped up and put into a waste paper bin. Somehow, that information found its way to the press. It was assumed that a cleaner or someone working for cleaning contractors in the set of chambers was responsible for removing the documents and passing them to the newspaper through a third party. John and his lawyers wished to know the source of the information.

At first instance, the judge ordered the newspaper to reveal the source. The Court of Appeal allowed the newspaper's appeal. The case is significant because the Court of Appeal took the view that the trial judge had overreacted. He had been concerned to ensure that the lawyer/client relationship was not undermined and, thus, confidence in the system would be maintained. However, in the Court of Appeal, the Master of the Rolls thought that there were more efficacious ways in which the relationship could be strengthened without reducing the protection offered to the press by section 10. The solution: first, to buy a shredding machine for the office and, second, to use it!

Having disposed of this case, we now come to a sequence of cases that currently define the legal position regarding section 10. The cases in question are:

- *Ashworth Hospital Authority v. MGN Ltd [2002] UKHL 29*
- *Financial Times & Others v. Interbrew SA [2002] EWCA Civ 274*
- *Mersey Care NHS Trust v. Ackroyd [2006] EWHC 107 (QB).*

For the details of the above cases, see Part Four.

The *Ashworth* case resulted in the House of Lords confirming the decisions of the High Court and Court of Appeal, which were that the source should be named. I would commend this statement of principle from Laws LJ taken from the Court of Appeals decision [2000] EWCA 334 at para 101:

the true position is that it is always prima facie ... contrary to the public interest that press sources should be disclosed; and in any given case the debate which follows will be conducted upon the question whether there is an overriding public interest, amounting to a pressing social need, to which the need to keep press sources confidential should give way.

Note, too, the importance attached to the non-disclosure of medical records in the Ackroyd case. You may wish to quote Lord Woolf, who gave the principal judgment in the House of Lords (para 6):

The situation here is exceptional ... as it has to be, if disclosure of sources is to be justified ... The source's disclosure was wholly inconsistent with the security of the records and the disclosure was made worse because it was purchased by a cash payment.

The intermediary from whom the *Daily Mirror* reporter purchased the clinical notes for Ian Brady, the Moors Murderer, was Robin Ackroyd. He refused to name his source within the hospital. The hospital then sought an order requiring him to do so. Gray J held that he need not do so. The decision appears to have been predicated on pragmatic grounds. The judge was confident that, with the passage of time (some six years), the health trust would gain little and achieve even less if Ackroyd was forced to reveal the name of his source (see Part Four for more details).

In the *Interbrew* case, a large, multinational brewing group wished to identify the source of confidential financial information leaked to national newspapers. The impact of publication was to cause the company's share price to fluctuate wildly. The Court of Appeal ordered the information retained by the *Financial Times* and other newspapers to be released. As Sedley LJ stated (para 55):

The public interest in protecting the source of such a leak is in my judgment not sufficient to withstand the countervailing public interest in letting Interbrew seek justice in the courts against the source.

In conclusion, it is probably accurate to assert that, despite the recent cases where the courts have been prepared to order journalists to reveal their sources, the courts have not abrogated the principle that it is, prima facie, against the public interest that press sources should be revealed. You may also wish to make the point that the *Interbrew* litigation ended with the company refusing to spend any more money trying to track down the source. The newspapers had indicated that they were prepared to take the case all the way to the European Court of Human

Rights and that would have involved the company in enormous expense. As far as I'm aware the source was never identified.

In February 2004, Lord Saville, the Chairman of the inquiry into the Bloody Sunday shootings, decided not to take action against three journalists who refused to name the sources of their stories. In Lord Saville's view, further legal action would not produce any new information of value to the inquiry and would only delay its completion. The result was perhaps understandable press elation at the decision and ITN went on record to hail it as a 'legal landmark' and a 'recognition of the rights of journalists to protect the identity of their sources.' You may wish to consider if that had ever been in doubt! You may also wish to argue that the Saville decision, taken together with the *Ackroyd* judgment, gives greater cause for optimism than at any time since the Contempt of Court Act came into force.

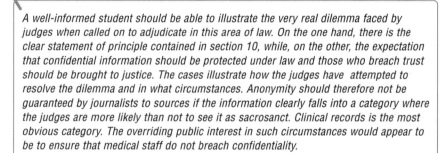

A well-informed student should be able to illustrate the very real dilemma faced by judges when called on to adjudicate in this area of law. On the one hand, there is the clear statement of principle contained in section 10, while, on the other, the expectation that confidential information should be protected under law and those who breach trust should be brought to justice. The cases illustrate how the judges have attempted to resolve the dilemma and in what circumstances. Anonymity should therefore not be guaranteed by journalists to sources if the information clearly falls into a category where the judges are more likely than not to see it as sacrosanct. Clinical records is the most obvious category. The overriding public interest in such circumstances would appear to be to ensure that medical staff do not breach confidentiality.

Other legislative considerations

When investigating alleged criminal activity, the police may wish to have access to information held by a media organisation. Your examiners may ask you to consider if you have the legal right to refuse to hand over material. Photography is one obvious area of media activity in which the police are likely to have an ongoing interest. You will need to refer to certain provisions in the Police and Criminal Evidence Act 1984 (PACE). The Act divides journalistic material into two categories. The first is termed 'excluded material' and the second 'special procedure.'

Journalistic material is defined in the Act as 'material acquired or created for the purposes of journalism.' Such material, *which must be held in confidence,* will normally be excluded from any search warrant the police are serving on a media organisation. Everyday photographic material from broadcasters and print media would not normally qualify as having the necessary quality of confidence to be protected under this legislation.

For journalistic material that doesn't qualify to be excluded, an application must be made to a circuit judge and, providing the following can be shown, an order is likely to be granted. The criteria are:

- *reasonable grounds* exist for believing that a *serious* arrestable offence has been committed *and*
- the material is likely to be of *substantial* value to the investigation *and*
- that material will, in all probability, constitute relevant evidence.

Of course, as with many things relating to the media, it should be in the *public interest* that the material be produced. The court will have to take account of the benefit likely to accrue to the investigation if the material is obtained and the circumstances under which the person in possession of the material holds it (see section 14 and Schedule 1 of PACE).

The dilemma facing a judge looking at such a situation is probably best expressed (at least for examination purposes) by reference to two cases.

In *R. v. Crown Court at Lewes, ex parte Hill (1991) 93 Crim. App.R.60, (at p. 61)* Bingham LJ spoke of the:

> public interest in the effective investigation and prosecution of crime and secondly in protecting personal and property rights of citizens against infringement and invasion.

Clearly, as the House of Lords said in *R. v. Southwark Crown Court, ex parte Bowles [1998] 2 All ER 193 [1998] UKHL 16,* endorsing the observation of Lloyd LJ in *Maidstone Crown Court, ex parte Watt [1988] Crim. LR 384:*

> The special procedure under ... Schedule 1 is a serious inroad upon the liberty of the subject. The responsibility for ensuring that the procedure is not abused lies with circuit judges. It is of cardinal importance that circuit judges should be scrupulous in discharging that responsibility. (At p. 23 per Lord Hutton)

The strong message is that circuit judges should not simply acquiesce to what the police or security services say amount to reasonable grounds and grant them a production order. The protection accorded to journalistic material will depend on circuit judges recognising the corresponding public interest in supporting freedom of expression and permitting journalists to retain documents in their possession. Two excellent examples to cite while attempting to illustrate the difficulty for the media are:

- *R. v. Bright, Alton and Rusbridger [2001] 1WLR 662*
- *BBC v. United Kingdom (1996) 21 EHRR CD 93.*

It is likely that, when considering this issue, you will be referred to other pieces of legislation on which the police and security services can rely when seeking to obtain evidence in the possession of journalists. Space does not permit a detailed examination of these provisions, but note in particular the following.

- Official Secrets Act 1989 and the House of Lords decision in *R. v. Shayler [2002] UKHL 11.*
- Police Act 1997.
- Regulation of Investigatory Powers Act 2000.
- Terrorism Act 2000. If a person believes or suspects that another has committed an offence and that information has come into his or her possession in the course of 'trade profession, business or employment', then, if he or she doesn't reveal the information to the police 'as soon as is reasonably practicable', he or she commits an offence (Sections 15–19).

The relevant offences are:

- funding terrorism
- money laundering
- using money or property for terrorist purposes.

This last piece of legislation does not appear to have created problems for the media so far, but no doubt a test case will be brought before too long. It is inevitable that investigative journalists' attention is at some stage going to be drawn to information regarding those offences, in which case they appear to be under a statutory duty to reveal their information to the police.

The protection of journalists' sources is a topic often examined in two parts. The first dealing with the interpretation of section 10 and when disclosure of the name of a source is 'necessary', the second considering documentary or other evidence in the possession of the media and what, if anything, can be done to resist applications from the police or security forces for access.

2.8	
privacy and breach of confidentiality	

Core Areas

- Law relating to confidentiality
- cases reflecting development of law
- Post-Human Rights Act developments
- Confidentiality and privacy

This is a hot topic and is likely to remain so as the English courts grapple with the implications of the European Court of Human Rights' decision in the *Caroline* case. Whatever the outcome of cases from now on, there will always be a place on a media law syllabus for this topic. The interest stems, in part, from the fact that, in this country, we do not have a separate tort of privacy. If we did, this might accord with our rights as expressed by Article 8 of the European Convention on Human Rights, but would seemingly be contrary to freedom of expression, which the media is so anxious to protect under Article 10.

There are those, both in positions of authority and not, who would welcome the heat being taken off them when they have committed the little and not so little indiscretions that the tabloids are so keen to highlight. We constantly hear from politicians that their private lives should be kept separate from their public personas.

The government is loath to legislate on this matter for fear of being accused of acting contrary to the interests of a free press and, therefore, in an anti-democratic way. The practical problem it faces, however, is massive. Exactly what would privacy rights encompass? If two adults voluntarily embark on an adulterous affair, is that really any of the general public's business? However, if one party to the relationship is a cabinet minister and the other a prominent socialite, does it then become our business? If a celebrity is taking lunch in a popular restaurant, then should she be able to prevent the media from publishing her photograph together with that of her companion? The absence of a discrete body of law dealing with privacy was never more graphically illustrated than in the case of *Kaye v. Robertson [1991] FSR 62.* Thus, Glidewell LJ opined:

It is well known that in English law there is no right to privacy and accordingly there is no right of action for breach of a person's privacy. The facts of the present case are a graphic illustration of the desirability of Parliament considering whether and in what circumstances statutory provision can be made to protect the privacy of individuals.

He was not alone in his views. Bingham LJ said (Quoted with approval in *Douglas & Another v. Northern & Shell plc [2000] EWCA 353 at para. 113 and 114):*

This case nonetheless highlights, yet again, the failure of both the common law of England and statute to protect in an effective way the personal privacy of individual citizens.

The third judge in the case, Leggatt LJ, thought that such a right 'can be recognised only by the legislature.'

There you have it in a nutshell. Should the flexibility of the common law permit the introduction of a 'new' branch of the law, in much the same way that it did in 1932 when Lord Atkin developed new principles of negligence into the law of tort, or should it be left to Parliament to make what is clearly perceived by some judges to be a necessary fundamental shift in legislation, which can, in fact, only be accomplished by Parliament?

You will have gathered from this brief introduction that numerous questions of this type can be raised. It will be your task to analyse whether or not the current law is balanced in favour of the media or the person or organisation complaining about the apparent intrusion into their private affairs.

How to structure your analysis

The approach I would recommend is, first, become familiar with the law relating to *confidentiality*. The protection offered by this branch of the law is well established and dates back to the famous case of *Prince Albert v. Strange [1849] 64 ER 293*. If you would like a quick yet authoritative guide to this case, then see Lord Hoffman's speech in *Campbell v. MGN Ltd [2004] UKHL 22*. The salient points are:

- 'the equitable action of breach of confidence ... has long been recognised as capable of being used to protect privacy'
- the *Prince Albert* case was deemed to be a 'seminal' decision
- the action could be used to 'protect privacy in the sense of preserving confidentiality of personal information', but was 'not founded on the notion that such information was in itself entitled to protection'

- as breach of confidence was an equitable remedy, the action did not 'depend on the personal nature of the information or extent of the publication but upon whether a confidential relationship existed between the person who imparted the information and the person who received it'
- therefore, in the *Prince Albert* case, the cause of action was based 'upon the defendant's actual or constructive knowledge of the confidential relationship between the Prince Consort and the printer to whom he had entrusted the plates of his etchings'.

Second, you might care to dip into the Law Commission's report on breach of confidence (Law Commission 110, 1974, Cmnd 8388) Clearly it is somewhat dated, but at least it will give you an impression of the issues that were, at the time, considered important.

Third, you need to build a list of significant cases that you might cite as reflecting the development of the law over the last 30 years. The question always to bear in mind is, 'To what extent can the law of confidentiality *adequately* provide a remedy for what might today be considered a breach of privacy?' The following are the key cases in this regard:

- *Coco v. A. N. Clark (Engineers) Ltd [1968] FSR 415*
- *Fraser v. Evans [1969] 1 All ER 8*
- *Woodward v. Hutchings [1977] 2 All ER 751*
- *Francombe v. Mirror Group [1984] 2 All ER 408*
- *Stephens v. Avery [1988] 2 All ER 477*
- *Barrymore v. News Group Newspapers [1997] FSR 600*
- *Archer v. Williams [2003] EWHC 1670.*

Let me quickly summarise the main issues arising from these cases. In the first, you need to consider the three elements deemed necessary by Megarry J to underpin an action for confidentiality. They are:

- the information required to have the necessary 'quality of confidence'
- the circumstances in which the information was obtained must have 'imported' an obligation of confidence
- unauthorised use must have been made of the information and this must be detrimental to the person who initially held and then imparted the information.

From the second case, simply use the words of Lord Denning MR to the effect that:

It [the law on confidence] depends on the broad principle of equity that he who has received information in confidence shall not take unfair advantage of it.

Note the word 'information'. There is no indication that the law is trying to protect people's privacy as opposed to providing a remedy for what amounts to a breach of trust.

The third case is important. It is one of the first 'celebrity' cases, but is still firmly based on actual or assumed breach of trust. The case is notable for two comments made by Lord Denning. The first is:

> *In these cases of confidential information it is a question of balancing the public interest in maintaining the confidence against the public interest in knowing the truth.*

The second is:

> *In this case the balance comes down in favour of the truth being told, even if it should involve some breach of confidential information.*

Please bear this in mind later when considering the *Campbell* case. *Woodward v. Hutchins* has not passed without critical comment, but perhaps it has been put most succinctly by Gummow J in the Australian case of *S.K. & F. v. Department of Community Services [1990] FSR 617 (p. 663)*:

> *An examination of the recent English decisions shows that the so-called 'public interest' defence is not so much a rule as an invitation to judicial idiosyncrasy by deciding each case on an ad hoc basis as to whether, on the facts overall, it is better to respect or to override the obligation of confidence.*

The fourth case concerned illegal telephone tapping and the taped conversations of Johnny Francombe, the National Hunt champion jockey, that came eventually into the possession of the *Daily Mirror*. He sought an injunction to prevent the *Daily Mirror* from publishing the information. There was no question that the tapping was a criminal offence under the Wireless Telegraphy Act 1949. The Court of Appeal held that the *Daily Mirror* was not entitled to publish on the basis that the public interest justified a breach of the criminal law. The public interest would have been served by making the tapes available to the police or Jockey Club. Publication would only serve the *Daily Mirror*'s interests, not the public interest.

The fifth case confirmed that 'three requirements have to be satisfied before a court will protect information as being legally confidential.' In other words, the three factors determined by Megarry J in the *Coco* case still prevailed. Judicial discretion, said Sir Nicolas Brown-Wilkinson, would not be exercised in favour of a claimant if the subject matter was 'merely trivial'. However, the exercising of such discretion could only be decided in light of all the circumstances. To be capable of protection, the information must have the 'basic attribute of inaccessibility.'

The next case appeared significant at the time. Television personality Michael Barrymore was the subject of a 'kiss and tell' exposé by one Paul Wincott, who claimed to have had sexual relations with the star. Jacobs J said:

> When people kiss and later one of them tells, the second person is almost certainly breaking a confidential relationship ... in this case the article went into detail about the relationship and crossed the line into arguable breach of confidence.

Barrymore's application for an injunction to prevent publication was granted. This follows the trend adopted by the court in *Stephens v. Avery*, that 'confidential relationships' are not to be viewed as exclusively linked to the marriage relationship. This decision must now be read in light of the Court of Appeal decision in *A v. B & C [2002] EWCA Civ 337*. Your attention is drawn to the comment by Lord Woolf CJ, para. 3 of his judgment, to the effect that:

> Since the coming into force of the Human Rights Act 1998 there has been an increase in the number of actions in which injunctions are being sought to protect the claimants from the publication of articles in newspapers on the grounds that the articles contain confidential information concerning the claimants, the publication of which, it is alleged, would infringe their privacy. Such actions can be against any part of the media.

He then goes on to set the scene for the post-Human Rights Act developments of, first, linking confidentiality with privacy and, now, the issue of whether or not, in light of the decision in the *Caroline* case, the establishment of a separate tort of privacy is not far away.

Finally, to the last in this group of cases, Lady Mary Archer, wife of the disgraced peer, Lord Archer of Weston-super-Mare, was deemed not to be a 'public figure' and entitled to an injunction and damages of £2,500 from her former personal assistant who had revealed personal information about her former employer. The judge held that Article 10 did not override her right to protect information relating to her private life.

When writing about the law on confidentiality, stress the following points:

- equitable remedy
- well-established area of law
- three major elements relating to confidential information
- protection not originally offered for what today we might regard as respect for family and private life
- types of relationship that will be regarded as confidential now gone beyond the bounds of marriage – in other words, personal information can be protected in addition to that which may be commercially sensitive
- information that is extremely trivial is unlikely to be protectable
- the existence of an obligation of confidence will depend on the circumstances
- the unauthorised use of confidential information may be justified as being in the public interest, which, in itself, means that a balancing exercise will need to take place in light of all the circumstances of the case.

Post-Human Rights Act developments

In respect of the most recent developments, you will be expected to consider the following.

- Is it possible to 'stretch' the law on confidentiality any further to encompass privacy issues? To put it another way, should confidentiality be confined within its traditional sphere of operation?
- Why is there a reluctance on the part of government to create legislation defining privacy rights?
- Consider how the judiciary have grasped the opportunity to apply the *Caroline* principles to this jurisdiction. This part will require you to examine the latest case law from both Europe and England and Wales.

Analysis

There are judicial pronouncements to the effect that the law on confidence is already stretched to breaking point. There are also judicial statements that suggest a law on privacy now exists. The strongest statement in support of the proposition probably comes from Sedley LJ in *Douglas & Another v. Northern & Shell PLC and Another [2002] EWCA Civ 353*. He says (para. 110):

> Nevertheless, we have reached the point at which it can be said with confidence that the law recognises and will appropriately protect a right of personal privacy.

He offers two reasons for this view. First, 'equity and the common law are today in a position to respond to an increasingly invasive social environment by affirming that everybody has a right to some private space.' Second, the Human Rights Act 1998 requires the courts to give appropriate effect to the right to respect for private and family life, as set out in Article 8. This results in a 'positive obligation to respect privacy … [and this] arguably gives the final impetus to the recognition of a right of privacy in English law.'

Sedley LJ's fellow judges, while acknowledging the argument, were less forthcoming. For example, you might like to quote Keene LJ, who felt that breach of confidence had 'now developed into something different from the commercial and employment relationships with which confidentiality is mainly concerned.'

Space does not permit a detailed analysis here of the many cases that have emerged since the Human Rights Act went on to the statute books. I would thus urge you to look for statements of principle in the following cases:

- *Douglas & Others v. Hello & Others [2003] EWHC 786 (Ch)*
- *Wainwright & Another v. Home Office [2003] UKHL 53*
- *Campbell v. MGN Ltd [2004] UKHL 22*
- *Von Hannover v. Germany [2004] EMLR 379*
- *Douglas v. Hello Ltd [2005] EWCA Civ 595*
- *McKennitt v. Ash [2005] EWHC 3003 (QB)*
- *HRH The Prince of Wales v. Associated Newspapers Ltd (No. 3) [2006] EWHC 522 (Ch)*
- *Wainwright v. United Kingdom [2006] ECHR 807.*

Here, briefly, are the points to note from these cases.

In *Douglas [2003]*, Lindsay J declined the invitation to recognise a law of privacy for five reasons (see Part Four or para. 229 of the judgment). Of particular importance is the third reason. The task of filling whatever 'privacy' gaps exist should rest with Parliament. The judge acknowledges that Parliament has so far failed to 'grasp the nettle', but that doesn't mean it will not have to be grasped in the future. His opinion is that parliamentary intervention is far preferable to 'the courts creating the law bit by bit at the expense of litigants and with the inevitable delays and uncertainty'.

In *Wainwright* (not a media case and one in which the events took place before the Human Rights Act came into force), the House of Lords emphatically declined to accept that privacy (as opposed to confidentiality) was part of the common law prior to the Human Rights Act. Lord Hoffman was prepared to accept that privacy was a 'value' underpinning the existence of the rule of law. However, that was a far cry from identifying privacy as a 'principle of law in itself.' Lord Scott would not be drawn on whether or not, if the events had occurred after the Human Rights Act had come into force, there could have been a successful action for breach of privacy.

Campbell, once again, illustrated the lack of enthusiasm by the judiciary for the creation of a new tort of privacy to fill in the gaps left by other remedies, principally breach of confidence.

Von Hannover offers – the *Caroline* case – a scintilla of hope that if Germany's 'privacy' laws were deemed inadequate in 'everyday situations', then so must our laws. The burning question immediately after the judgment was whether or not the government here would be forced to act in the near future. Remember, Lindsay J in *Douglas* thought it arguable that countries such as Germany 'have apparently workable laws of privacy' and yet the European court held them to be inadequate.

The answer to the question is no! That response has not pleased the judiciary and, as a result, the judges have made their feelings known. The Court of Appeal in *Douglas [2005]* felt constrained by precedent and confined any remedies available to breach of confidence. However, please note the words of Lords Phillips MR (para. 53):

> The court should, in so far as it can, develop the action for breach of confidence in such a manner as will give effect to both Article 8 and Article 10 rights.

That is the 'precedent' commitment, yet, two lines further on, he says:

> We cannot pretend that we find it satisfactory to be required to shoehorn within the cause of action of breach of confidence claims for publication of unauthorised photographs of a private occasion.

That would seem to indicate a wish on behalf of the Court of Appeal that breach of confidence actions should centre on confidential *information* only, irrespective of whether or not it is of a personal or commercial nature.

Perhaps spurred on by this ruling, the High Court in the *McKennitt* case seems to have made a quantum leap in acknowledging a cause of action for breach of privacy outside the bounds of breach of confidence. Please pay particular attention to what appears to be a statement of principle (para. 57), when the judge refers to the 'significant shift' taking place away from Article 10 in favour of protecting citizens' Article 8 rights (see Part Four for more details of this case). Also, note that, on 25 May 2006, the Court of Appeal gave leave to Ash to appeal on the basis that the case raised a number of important legal issues and as yet unresolved issues that required scrutiny by the Court of Appeal.

That theme was then picked up by Blackburne J in the *HRH The Prince of Wales* case (see in particular para 120 and 121; see also Part Four for more details).

Conclusion

You may wish to conclude that the law on privacy is both crystal clear and, at the same time, confused. What *is* clear is that no general tort of privacy exists in this jurisdiction. Neither Parliament nor the House of Lords has acted to create such a tort. What is *also* clear is that the law on confidentiality will be applicable in a number of privacy situations, as demonstrated by the *Douglas* and *Campbell* decisions, but for how long?

What stills remains to be resolved is whether or not the 'significant shift' that appears to be taking place in favour of Article 8 rights at the time of writing will continue. If it does, will, ultimately, the House of Lords act to introduce clear privacy principles in the same way that it did in 1932 when establishing the tort of negligence (*Donoghue v. Stevenson*)?

It has been suggested that the 'law of privacy has metamorphosed from being concerned with the misuse of private information into taking account of intrusion into an individual's private life' (Press Association News Bulletin, 4 March 2005). If this is true, perhaps we will hear less about the law of privacy and more about the new law of intrusion!

As a final point, you may wish to include in an answer reference to the decision in New Zealand in *Hosking v. Runting [2004] NZCA 34*. The Court of Appeal decided, by a 3:2 majority, to recognise a freestanding tort of privacy. The court, albeit by a bare majority, believed that greater clarity would be achieved by analysing confidence and privacy as separate causes of action as they were different concepts and to link them would simply cause confusion. If it can be done in the Antipodes, why not here?

2.9

elements of intellectual property law

Core Areas

- Image rights
- Copyright
- Passing off
- Trademarks

This topic may well figure in your course, subject to the amount of time available, and might be construed as more important and relevant under the media law rubric. This is because the subject matter of at least one element of intellectual property law is extensive and, arguably, cannot be considered in any meaningful depth in the time available. The Copyright, Designs and Patents Act 1988 runs to 306 sections, without the schedules, and then there are also the changes that have been introduced by both UK and European legislation to take into account!

I need to make an assumption at this point. If *I* were offering this topic as part of a media course, I would be inclined to discuss the issues within the overall framework of image rights. The reason for this is that it is an increasingly important area of law because, as with privacy, there is no discrete body of law relating to image rights in the UK. Therefore, in order to provide some protection, the Core Areas mentioned above have to be harnessed.

This is, therefore, the approach I will adopt here, so I apologise now if that is not the way your tutor approaches the subject.

Image rights

The basic assumption is that a person's image may have a potential value in the marketplace. In one sense, it is the equivalent of the

American 'right of publicity' – a right that does not exist in this country. The theory is that an individual has the exclusive right to control commercial use and exploitation of his or her image, voice and likeness. In other words, image rights can be viewed as a commercial property right.

It will be obvious that image rights could, then, be viewed as being part of a discrete law on privacy, except for the fact we do not have a tort of privacy in this country. However, Article 8 provides that everyone has a right to respect for their private and family lives and, therefore, the unauthorised taking and (mis)using of a person's image may ultimately be considered to be part of the protection offered by Article 8, with suitable remedies flowing from that fact ... but not just yet.

So, to protect one's image from commercial exploitation, one may fall back on the *law of copyright.* This is essentially a 'negative' right, which seeks to prevent others from making copies of the work of an author or creator. Let us take two examples relating to images.

In *Peck v. United Kingdom [2003] 36 EHHR41,* the question was, 'What rights did the owner of the CCTV pictures showing him attempting to commit suicide have over the commercial exploitation of the film?' Ultimately, the European Court concluded that the laws in this country did not give sufficient legal remedies to Peck when the images of him were sold on to British television and transmitted.

The balancing exercise, then, is between the rights of the copyright owner and the Article 8 rights of the individual caught on film.

In the *Elizabeth Jagger* case in March 2005, a temporary injunction was granted by Bell J preventing the unauthorised use of CCTV film showing her in a compromising position with Calum Best in a nightclub at 4 a.m. However, at the time of writing, it appears that she has bought the rights to the CCTV footage from the club and is therefore protecting her own property interests in the film by resorting to the law on copyright. Whether or not Jagger will still be able to invoke the law on privacy or confidentiality to protect her image when, in fact, she could put the images on the Internet (and take any profit) remains to be seen.

For more information on this area of the law, visit the Information Commissioner Office website at www.informationcommissioner.gov.uk and look at the code of practice that covers images on CCTV.

I would suggest that you gather together basic information about the following aspects of the law, together with any recent examples from the courts.

Copyright

There are a number of sources of information on the subject of copyright accessible via the Internet and they will give you the basic grounding you need to apply copyright principles to situations likely to arise in a media law course. The UK Patent Office's website at www.patent.gov. uk includes FAQs on its copyright section. There is a checklist of fundamental questions that are given straightforward answers. For example, in response to the question, 'What is copyright?' you are informed that:

- there is no official register for copyright
- copyright comes into effect immediately, as soon as something that can be protected is created
- there are types of works that copyright seeks to protect
- copyright does not protect ideas, but does protect the way the ideas are expressed in a piece of work.

Another useful source of information about copyright is to be found at www.intellectual-property.gov.uk while Wikipedia's site at http://en. wikipedia.org/wiki/Copyright_law_of_the_United-Kingdom has a slightly more detailed exposition of the basic law.

An enlightening case that covers a number of issues likely to arise in this context is *The Right Honourable Paddy Ashdown MP PC v. Telegraph Group Ltd [2001] EWCA Civ 1142*. The case centred on the contention by the Telegraph Group that, when considering whether or not an actionable breach of copyright had occurred, due regard should be given to Article 10 of the European Convention. It also raised issues connected with the Criticism and Review section of the Copyright, Designs and Patents Act 1988 (fair dealing, under section 30). The case also deserves attention because it provides comments on the nature, restrictions and remedies relating to copyright. The case law that will be relevant to your analysis and which is discussed includes:

- *BBC v. BSB Ltd [1992] Ch 141*
- *Pro Sieben Media AG v. Carlton UK Television [1999] 1 WLR 605*
- *Time Warner v. Channel 4 Television [1994] EMLR 1.*

See also the case of *The Newspaper Licensing Agency v. Marks & Spencer [2000] EWCA Civ 179.*

Passing off

English law recognises the common law tort of passing off. This is designed to enable a trader to protect the goodwill that a business enjoys. It may be an obvious point to make, but 'goodwill' is often intangible. It is something that exists in the minds of individuals, linking them, positively, to a particular product or organisation.

Passing off as an action may apply to situations where trademark protection does not apply. If a registered trademark applies, the owner may sue in passing off as well as for infringement of his or her trademark.

Adopting the approach mentioned above, I suggest that you identify a suitably recent passing off case in order to discover the legal issues connected with this action. A good one to read is *Irvine & Others v. Talk Sport Radio Ltd [2003] EWCA Civ 423.*

Trademarks

Registered trademarks guarantee the origin of goods and services and the process operates within the terms of the Trade Marks Act 1994. The legislation also implements European directives on the topic. Section 1 defines a 'trademark' as:

> any sign capable of being represented graphically which is capable of distinguishing goods and services of one undertaking from those of another.

Section 2 goes on to state that a registered trademark is a property right obtained by the registration of the trademark and the proprietor has the rights and remedies provided under the Act and these, of course, will include injunctions and damages.

Conclusion

This part of the book has highlighted the major components of typical media law syllabuses. You will have appreciated that a successful outcome to any standard form of assessment will depend largely upon you identifying the key legal principle and providing supporting legal authority. My view is that you should always focus on the primary sources because it is through case law that you are best able to understand how judges have reached their decisions. Reference to secondary sources adds the 'gloss' to any answer because it is the job of lawyers and academics to analyse judgments and try to find any points of criticism. Finally, remember from the outset of your course to try as far as possible to avoid purely 'descriptive' answers. Forego those in favour of answers with a high level of judicial comment and appropriate analysis.

part three

study and revision skills

- Introduction
- Lectures
- Seminars and tutorials
- Terminology
- Essay writing
- Revision hints and tips
- Examination hints and tips
- Good luck

3.1

introduction

The aim of this part of the book is to give practical advice on how to approach your study and thereby gain maximum benefit from your course and the best marks possible in any assessment procedures.

Having been in this business for more years than I care to recall, I can say with some degree of authority that no two people study in exactly the same way. Different people will have differing levels of motivation, ambition and commitment, so if I try to give generic advice on how to study, my efforts will not resonate with many of you. 'After all,' you are likely to say, 'we have been studying since the age of three and it is probably too late to make dramatic changes to our study methodology simply because we are at university.'

Therefore, in terms of approach to lectures and tutorials, I intend to give the briefest of advice. You will make your own decisions on how to approach these sessions. The variables will include the time of day, the effectiveness and competence of your lecturer and the *perceived* benefit from engaging in this activity. I recall a number of years ago being a member of a quality assurance panel, sent to examine the delivery of law at one of the UK's top universities. We found standards to be excellent and, in particular, rated the lectures as being outstanding. If I recall correctly, the disappointment (to us) was that only some 25 per cent of eligible students chose to attend!

3.2

lectures

As most of you will be new to the study of law, the first thing to do is come to terms with the court structure and appropriate legal terminology.

Your lecturer should go through both elements. Do take note because this is important to the way you communicate in coursework and examinations. It is always worth pointing out the *level* at which a decision was made. For example, when talking about the *Reynolds* decision on qualified privilege, point out that it was a *landmark House of Lords* decision, the principles of which have been *applied* subsequently in a number of other cases. Too many students might simply write, 'In *Reynolds v. Times Newspapers Ltd* ... the Irish Prime Minister resigned. In other words, they go straight into the facts of the case without stating its importance or, in fact, it's chronology, coming as it did just after the Human Rights Act 1998 came on to the statute book. In lectures you should think about the *significance* of a case when the lecturer mentions it.

The next point about listening and observing at lectures is to not forget the legal *context* in which the discussion is taking place. Law lecturers are obsessed with case law. A standard lecture may well include references to perhaps 15–20 cases. You cannot be expected to read up on all these cases and nor should you. It may be that these cases are quoted as a means of illustrating how the courts have interpreted a statute. If so, prior to considering the case, think about the following.

- What was the purpose or objective in Parliament passing the legislation in the first place?
- Once this has been determined, you are in a better position to understand what the courts are trying to achieve by interpreting the case the way they have. For example, when considering section 10 of the Contempt of Court Act 1981, the wording of the section leads one to conclude that Parliament was seeking to protect free speech and journalists' sources, *but* not at all costs. Appreciate that point and you will be better able to understand the balancing exercise undertaken by the courts in cases such as *Ashworth*, *Interbrew* and *Ackroyd*, discussed in Part Two.

The issues raised in lectures are pointers that provide direction in relation to each segment of your course (see Part One). The assumption is that you will build on what you have been told in lectures, so you should never (assuming you want good marks) think merely writing out the bare bones of the lecture material to hand in as coursework will suffice.

3.3

seminars and tutorials

Like most things in life, it is a good idea to know at the outset what the purpose of the exercise is. Will it be simply an hour spent expanding on the information given in the lectures? Are there tutorial sheets with problem questions to consider? After the first session, have you discovered that the tutor does most of the talking and you are simply his or her audience? Do you have the opportunity to ask questions and seek clarification about points that you don't understand? Are they stimulating and involving or boring and irrelevant or somewhere in between?

Your perception will determine how much preparation you do for the class. Most students, in my experience, attend tutorials because they feel that they will learn something *and* the learning will ultimately help them with their *assessment*. Irrespective of how much time you spend trying to convince students that the information will indeed be helpful to their future careers or cerebral development, they still think first and foremost about how attending tutorials will help them succeed in the assessment process. I view that as a positive. Many of my colleagues wouldn't. They would see examining legal material in the context of how to deal with it for assessment purposes as in some way being anti-academic. It is not then the cerebral exercise it is supposed to be.

The trouble is, these same tutors also believe that students will be able to assimilate coursework and examination expectations by osmosis. Sadly, that is not the case for many students, who are ultimately disappointed with their examination results. The *methodology* of answering examination questions is still vital to success.

My tip is to try and gather from your tutor as much information as possible about *how* the particular topic under consideration might be dealt with in an examination. A tutorial sheet containing a number of problem questions from past examination papers that are then discussed in class will always be of benefit. Later in Part Three I will show you how to analyse problem questions.

Try to build relationships within your tutorial group. Some courses have group exercises, so to have a strong bond with a number of your colleagues should pay dividends if you are asked to work with them on pieces of group coursework. The theory here is that all members of the group should make an equal contribution to the presentation or written work and receive, in return, equal marks.

Tutorials should also help you to decide whether or not you really like the subject matter of the course you have chosen. In reality, it is too late to make a change, but it will help to increase your motivation if you really find the content of the course interesting. Media law ought never to be taught as simply an 'academic' subject. Over the months that you study media law, you will probably find that the courts have delivered a number of important decisions and, moreover, some of those decisions will attract some press interest. Therefore, you are actually reading in the newspapers about the laws you are studying and that helps to meld the 'academic' with 'real life'. *Galloway MP v. Telegraph Group Ltd* [2004] is a case in point.

The tutorials or seminars should provide you with a variety of views and opinions. You may have to defend your corner against attack from other students or the tutor.

Tutorials will invariably purport to deal with one large topic at a time – for example, defamation, contempt of court or privacy. Nevertheless, you should not assume that the law develops in simple categories. The tutorial should also be a venue where you can link other elements of the course to the topic under discussion. For example, you might link the law on prior restraint to defamation to breach of confidence and privacy. The topic under discussion may well be privacy, the context injunctions, while the issue to discuss that of the possibility of someone obtaining an injunction to prevent, say, a programme being broadcast on national television because it shows a celebrity doing embarrassing things, as in the *Jagger v. News Group Newspapers* case in 2005.

My advice on how to approach seminars is to prepare well, but not mechanically. Prior to the session, think about the issues that are raised by the problem or question on the tutorial sheet or those you might wish to raise once you are in the room.

Each group will contain students with differing levels of personal confidence. Those of you who are somewhat shy or less forthcoming than your colleagues will find prior preparation invaluable in persuading you to make a contribution to the class. In other words, you know what you want to say because you have done the research and you know that it is correct, so just wait for the moment to arrive when you can make your statement. If, as it should be, it is well received, this will give your self-confidence a boost. Of course, don't just have *one* thing prepared in advance. Ensure that you have three or four relevant things to say so that if you miss the moment first time, you will be ready for the second occasion.

As a rule of thumb, always try to quote from *primary sources* to back up your arguments. It's all very well quoting academics or other writers, but, ultimately, the comments that carry the most weight are those of the judiciary.

However, you will undoubtedly be referred to a number of secondary sources. They can *assist* you in attaining a high mark for your assessment. Look first at articles by leading practitioners and then at those written by academics. The articles written by lawyers are likely to give you a greater practical insight into the topics under investigation.

The **Articles** section of the www.5rb.co.uk website contains some excellent material. For example:

DEFAMATION

1 *Libel and publication in the Public Interest* by Desmond Browne QC. 2/12/2005

2 *Recent Practical issues in Defamation* by Desmond Browne QC. 26/1/2005

3 *Recent developments in Defamation* by David Sherbourne. 15/9/2004

PRIVACY

1 *A Review of recent developments in the law of privacy and the media* by Mark Warby QC. 26/1/2005.

2 *The Princess, the paparazzi and the press* by Matthew Nicklin. 15/7/2004.

COURT REPORTING

1 *Reporting the Courts* by Adam Wolanski. 13/3/2006

COPYRIGHT/IMAGE RIGHTS & TRADEMARKS

1 *Image rights and privacy after* Douglas v. Hello by Christina Michalos. 15/6/2005.

ACADEMIC SOURCES.
Perhaps the most obvious source is the Entertainment Law Review. For example:

BROADCAST REGULATION

1 *The Commission's proposals for a new directive on Audio Visual Content.* Oliver Castendyk and Kathrin Bottcher. (Ent LR 2006 17(6) pp 174–180).

PRIVACY

1 *A Review of the Law of Privacy* by Mark Lewis, Charlotte Hinton, Hugh Beverly-Smith and Geoff Hussey. (EntLR 2005 16 (7) pp 174–181)

You will also find case commentaries such as:

'Judge shows Beckham red card as nanny blows the whistle's by Helen Padley. (Ent LR 2005 16 (8) pp. 235–236.

Clearly one could list numerous articles in a range of academic journals. However, you must simply take your lead from your tutor given the reasonable expectation that he or she will refer you to the articles which they believe to be the most suitable.

I would however reiterate my view that the pecking order should be:

1 Primary sources i.e. case law

2 Articles by practitioners, particularly if they are specialists in the areas of law being studied

3 Articles by academics.

Finally, don't hesitate to take some notes in the tutorial to help develop your knowledge of the subject matter or assist you in remembering other people's opinions.

Tutorials and seminars can help build self-confidence as well as furthering your knowledge of the subject matter. They can help increase motivation and self-discipline if you really take a shine to the subject matter.

3.4

terminology

Lawyers have their own language. Sometimes modern, frequently archaic, it nevertheless needs to be appreciated, if not adopted, if you are going to do well in your assessment. It will serve you well if you accept from the outset that, when analysing a problem, you should consider the issues from a *neutral* perspective. What the lawyers call *authority* should support any conclusions. This will usually be a decision of a court in this country, overseas or the European Court of Human Rights. It may, on occasions, be the writings of an academic or lawyer, as published in a textbook or academic journal. Occasionally, it may be an official body, such as the Law Commission or a Select Committee of the House of Commons. In your lectures, you should make a note of sources that *you believe* will provide the *authority* you need to support analytical arguments at a later stage in your course.

Lawyers will also suggest that you do not be dogmatic. All lawyers are meant to help the court, irrespective of who they are representing. Therefore, you should practise writing:

- 'It is *submitted* that the *better view* is ...'
- 'The stronger argument *appears* to be ...'
- 'It is *suggested* that the *authorities support* the proposition that ...'
- 'The conclusion is that the *balance of authority lies in favour* of the claimant ...'

Once you have worked out the *precedent* issues, you will have appreciated that judges are given different titles depending on the court they are working in. Therefore, a trainee journalist attending Crown Court for the first time should note that the circuit judge who presides will be referred to as 'Judge', as in, *'At Cardiff Crown Court, Judge Stephen Hopkins sentenced the defendant to six years' imprisonment ...'*.

If you are reporting on the higher courts, then the nomenclature changes. A judge of the High Court is referred to as 'Justice' and, in the Court of Appeal, either 'Lord Justice' or 'Lady Justice'. Finally, in the House of Lords, the judges are known as 'Law Lords' with, currently, one exception – Baroness Hale of Richmond. So, you would write, for example, 'Lord Hoffman' or 'Baroness Hale'. Law students and media students studying at undergraduate level should use these titles in their coursework and examinations. It is simply sloppy to write, 'Hoffman said ...'. Even if you state correctly what he said, you are likely to lose marks for poor style and presentation.

3.5

essay writing

The essay writing that you will be asked to undertake will invariably be related to your assessment. There will be one essay of perhaps 2,500 words, its title chosen from a list of topics relevant to the nature of the material studied as part of the course. If your course covers two semesters, then, in all probability, you will be given the essay titles at the commencement of the second semester. Alternatively, they may have been included in the course outline provided at the beginning of the academic year.

The biggest single fault, in my experience, is that, in the introduction, students will seemingly do anything to avoid referring in their answer to the question set. They seem so anxious to start to write about the broad topic that they leave out the important points of saying *what* they intend to do and *why* they are even writing about it in the first place. Let me use an actual example so you can avoid this pitfall.

This question was motivated by the decision in the George Galloway libel action, the judgment to which was delivered in December 2004. It is a quotation extracted from a Media Guardian *article on 6 December 2004, four days after the decision. It was written by Dan Tench, a media partner of the law firm Olswang. Here is the quotation:*

The success last week of the libel action brought by former Labour MP George Galloway against the Daily Telegraph *will come as an unpleasant shock to the media. Not only did the judgment seem to dilute the celebrated 'Reynolds defence' to a libel action, much relied upon by newspapers when reporting matters considered to be in the public interest, but the damages awarded of £150,000 were astonishingly high. The judge's concerns about the* Telegraph's *reporting were perhaps understandable, but with these damages, the judge appears, at a stroke, to have undone many of the gains made by the media in libel law in the 1990s.*

Critically evaluate the above statement.

Approach

Start with the question, 'What have I been asked to do?'

Answer

- Write everything you know about defamation? (Wrong.)
- Write everything you know about the defence of common law qualified privilege? (Wrong.)
- Write everything you know about defamation and qualified privilege? (Wrong.)
- Write everything you know about defamation, qualified privilege and damages? (Wrong.)
- Approach the question in a step-by-step manner as follows? (Correct.)

Suggested approach

1 First of all, look at what the examiner expects you to do – that is, *evaluate* the statement and do so in a *critical* manner. Now, take a dictionary and find out what 'evaluate' and 'critical' mean.

2 'Evaluate' means to assess or appraise.

3 'Critical' means engaged in criticism, making or involving adverse or censorious comments or judgements.

4 So, you have to assess or appraise the quotation and, then, in light of your knowledge of the appropriate law, engage in criticism of the passage. You need to make judgments.

5 Therefore, in your introductory paragraph, make reference to what is expected of you. For example:

The question asks us to critically evaluate the Dan Tench statement. This quotation is taken from his immediate response to the Galloway decision in the High Court in December 2004. Having thought carefully about the passage, it appears to warrant evaluation at three levels. First, there is the contention that the celebrated 'Reynolds defence', has been diluted. Second, the comment is made that the damages awarded were 'astonishingly high'. This point will be evaluated. Finally, he comes to the conclusion that many media gains over the last 15 years have been 'undone' because of the decision. Taking the first point, ...

I hope that you are able to see the merit of commencing your essay answer in this way. You are communicating to the examiner that you are going to do exactly what is required of you by the question and that you have considered the statement and concluded there are three major elements to discuss. Great! You have created a mood of positive expectancy in the examiner that can only be to your advantage.

The examiner will also be impressed because there appears to be logic linking the various parts of the essay:

1 introduction

2 *Reynolds* and dilution

3 damages 'astonishingly high'

4 gains 'undone' over last 15 years

5 conclusion.

Let me, in note form, expand on parts 2–5 to show you what the rest of an excellent essay would look like.

Reynolds and dilution

- Importance of *Reynolds*, Human Rights Act, freedom of expression.
- *Reynolds* and precedent. Lower courts have to apply the principles as it's a House of Lords decision.
- What did Reynolds decide? Duty/interest principle. Responsible journalism. Lord Nicholls' ten non-exhaustive factors.
- Analysis of how Reynolds' principles were applied in *Galloway*. Why Eady J threw out the *Reynolds* defence with some disdain! (Don't be afraid of being critical because you have the judge – and now the Court of Appeal – to back you up!)
- Subconclusion: The principles remain the same, therefore have *not* been diluted. *Telegraph* was its own worst enemy in failing so comprehensively to match up to the *responsible journalism* standards.
- Be on the ball and mention that, in the later case of *Armstrong v. Times Newspapers [2004]*, the newspaper was not even allowed to plead the common law qualified privilege defence! (The decision was later overturned by the Court of Appeal.) Ask, rhetorically, what is happening when two of our major newspapers take a hammering in the High Court?

Damages 'astonishingly high'

- Key word is 'astonishingly', so how is that to be discussed? Current ceiling for damages for defamation is £200,000, so £150,000 – figure awarded – is only 75 per cent of the maximum permissible – hardly *astonishingly* high! See *Lillie & Reed v. Newcastle City Council [2002]*.

- Has been a punitive element in the award, given that *Telegraph* failed to satisfy most of Lord Nicholls' ten factors.
- *Telegraph failed* with defence of *fair comment* as well as qualified privilege and that factor may have added to level of award.
- Any compensatory award for defamation will be related to seriousness of libel. To allege that the activities of a British MP are tantamount to him being a traitor is pretty damaging as far as reputation goes!
- Set against awards since 1995 when the Court of Appeal established guide-lines for the assessment of damages, £150,000 *not* 'astonishingly high'. Maximum award in contested cases in 2003 was £65,000. In 2002, maximum was £200,000 in *Lillie* case. In 2001, £105,000 award upheld by Court of Appeal in *Kiam II v. MGN Ltd [2002] EWCA Civ 43*. An excellent case to mention as Court of Appeal reviews many authorities dealing with jury awards in defamation cases from 1992 onwards. In 2005, Rupert Lowe, the Chairman of Southampton Football Club, was awarded £250,000 – now that *was* astonishingly high!
- *SubConclusion*: Award may be on high side, but surely not *astonishingly* high. Case was heard by a single judge without a jury, so it can be assumed to reflect current practice.

Gains 'undone' over last 15 years

- Reference to the award culture in past – juries were free to award whatever they felt appropriate.
- Result – high awards invariably reduced by Court of Appeal. For example, award to Sonia Sutcliffe of £600,000 against *Private Eye* was reduced to £60,000 on appeal.
- Media made other gains in 1990s via the Defamation Act 1996. For example, introduction of offer of amends process and summary procedure both beneficial to the media. Neither of these is affected by *Galloway*.
- Futile to compare awards made ten years ago with those made today because the jury no longer has unfettered discretion to decide how much is appropriate. Judge will inform a jury of the 'brackets' within which he or she believes award should be placed. For example, 'somewhere between £20,000 and £40,000.' Jury does not have to agree with judge (see *Kiam II* and the recent *Purnell v. Business F1 Magazine* case in 2006).
- Subconclusion: Comment is not borne out by the facts.

Conclusion

You don't have to agree with the above, but, if you do, then you would submit that your analysis of *Galloway* does not fit the description offered by *The Guardian*. The fact that it took the newspaper some time to appeal against the decision would tend to support the conclusion that the judge got it right. Subsequently, the Court of Appeal decided that there was nothing wrong with his findings (January 2006). You might wish to make a tongue in cheek comment that the media are their own worst enemies at the moment and ponder on whether or not they have learned anything over the last six years. Your final point could be that the media lost in *Reynolds* because of sloppy journalism and they *still* lose because of sloppy journalism!

Some rules

Essay writing is a relatively straightforward exercise, provided you follow a few simple rules. The first is to address the question set. The second is to ensure that your answer is coherent. The more logical it is, the better. Third, make sure that there are *subconclusions* in your answer. By this simple expedient you will be able to demonstrate that you are always trying to address the question set. Throughout, too, use case authorities and, where appropriate, academic comment. Finally, ensure that you have an overall conclusion.

It is probably a good idea to avoid writing in the first person. In this way, you ensure that your tutor doesn't write on the essay 'and who are you in the pecking order?' Tutors prefer to read the views of judges and expert commentators rather than those of undergraduates who may have studied the law for no more than a few weeks. Just to be sure, ask your tutor what is the preferred writing style. You should also check to see if your tutor wishes you to add footnotes or give all case references in a bibliography at the end of the essay. You will normally be given advice on how to structure your essay, but, if you are not, then don't be afraid to ask.

One other piece of advice (that many of you will ignore) – do not leave writing the essay to the last moment. Computers crash, books are not available in the library and illness can, and sometimes does, intervene (that includes hangovers!)

When you have finished your final draft, leave it for at least 24 hours, then come back to it and proofread the work very carefully. Once satisfied, then complete the essay by adding the bibliography. The reason for leaving it for 24 hours is to let your brain forget what it *thinks* is there and instead notice what is *actually* written there. Favourites for correction are 'trial', which is frequently printed as 'trail', and 'principal', often confused with 'principle'.

Examples of essay questions to practise on

Journalists' sources and section 10 of the Contempt of Court Act 1981

Lord Saville's decision not to pursue an action for contempt of court against the Channel 4 news journalist Alex Thompson, producer Lena Ferguson and the *Daily Telegraph's* Toby Harndon for failing to identify their sources to the Bloody Sunday Inquiry was earlier this year hailed by ITN's Chief Executive, Mark Wood, as a 'legal landmark.' He went on to state:

> *Today's decision sets an important precedent. It is a rare example of the British courts upholding the rights of journalists and broadcasters to protect their sources in important matters of public interest.*

He went on to say that the decision:

> *redresses the balance in favour of investigative journalism.*

Taking into account appropriate judicial decisions over the last two decades, critically consider whether or not you believe the above assessment is over optimistic.

Intellectual property

> *'Image rights' do not exist per se in the United Kingdom, but are based upon a number of statutory rights, none of which are specifically designed to protect the unauthorised use of a personality's image.*
>
> *Andrew Braithwaite, Intellectual Property Partner, Osborne Clarke Solicitors, in house journal*

Critically consider the various legal measures that may be invoked when trying to protect image rights and assess how successful celebrities have been in attempting to legally protect their 'image' for commercial purposes.

3.6	
revision hints and tips	

Revision is very much a personal undertaking. The length of time devoted to it will vary from student to student. All students will, at some stage or another, proclaim that they do not have enough time! Lesson number one, therefore, is to ensure that you are good at time management. The amount of time devoted to a subject will invariably depend on how comfortable you feel about your knowledge of the subject matter.

For many, revision is about writing more notes, thereby taking on board more facts that inevitably will not reappear on the examination papers simply because you don't have enough time to regurgitate *all* the information you possess.

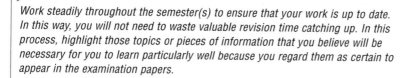

Work steadily throughout the semester(s) to ensure that your work is up to date. In this way, you will not need to waste valuable revision time catching up. In this process, highlight those topics or pieces of information that you believe will be necessary for you to learn particularly well because you regard them as certain to appear in the examination papers.

Familiarity with your material can help reduce anxiety, inspire confidence and fuel motivation – all of which help ensure that you turn in a good performance in the examinations.

Case law

As I mentioned in Part One, you need to highlight important case law as you progress through your course. You will be referred to an excessive amount of case law during your course, so you should determine which of those cases you are *bound* to have to use in your examinations – the five-star cases. You cannot discuss topics authoritatively without referring to key cases. Here are some to get you started.

Topic	Must mention
Prior restraint	*Cream Holdings*
	Martha Greene
Common law qualified privilege	*Reynolds*
	Galloway (High Court and Court of Appeal)
	Henry v. BBC (No. 2)
	Jameel
Privacy	*Campbell*
	Caroline
	McKennitt
	Prince Charles
And so on	

Primary sources

I have frequently mentioned the importance of primary sources. This includes legislation, statutory instruments, case law and, of course, the European Convention on Human Rights. The importance of legislation is simply that it will provide the context for your study of much of the law. Identify the major pieces of legislation that reflect the topics you have studied. Your list will probably include:

- Children and Young Persons Act 1933
- Contempt of Court Act 1981
- Broadcasting Act 1990
- Sexual Offences (Amendment) Act 1992
- Defamation Act 1996
- Human Rights Act 1998
- Sexual Offences Act 2003
- Courts Act 2003
- And so on ...

Then, for each piece of legislation, note the important sections as they have been interpreted by the courts. So, if it is the Human Rights Act and you are considering developments in the law on prior restraint, you would identify section 12 (freedom of expression) and subsection 3 in particular. You would then link it to *Cream Holdings Ltd & Others v. Banerjee & Others [2004]*, together with *Greene v. Associated Newspapers [2004]*.

You might then subdivide further by recognising the importance of the House of Lords' decision in *Cream Holdings* and compiling a number of short, but nevertheless significant, statements from the report. As an example, you might quote from Lord Nicholls, who gave the leading speech. His speech is packed with authoritative information right from the first paragraph. For example:

- section 12 makes special provision regarding freedom of expression
- the 'threshold test' that has to be satisfied under section 12(3)
- the case is concerned with the meaning of 'likely' in section 12(3)
- at the centre of the dispute is the unauthorised taking of 'confidential' material and whether or not it is in the 'public interest' that it should be published
- important authority: *American Cyanamid Co. v. Ethican Ltd [1975] AC 396*
- does 'likely' mean 'more likely than not' or 'probably'
- higher than 'real prospect', but a test that 'permits the court to dispense with this higher standard where particular circumstances make this necessary'
- 'there can be no single, rigid standard governing all applications for interim restraint orders'
- because of 'public interest' Cream's prospects at any future trial not sufficiently likely to justify making an interim restraint order in this case.

The above methodology ought to be employed on a continuous basis throughout the year in preparation for the commencement of revision. Failing that, perhaps a couple of weeks before you are going to start, dissect your notes and identify the critical cases and issues using the process illustrated above.

If you have done this, when you do start revising, you will be focussing on what is important. Please avoid the sponge-like tendency to absorb more and more *facts*. From an examination viewpoint, you will have little enough time to discuss the relevant law, let alone give a detailed assessment of the facts of each case you quote.

In addition to revising from and about primary sources, you will also be expected to refer to *secondary* material. These will be articles from various sources. Some may have appeared in well-established legal journals, such as the *Entertainment and Media Law Review* or *Modern Law*

Review. The *Guardian* newspaper's Media section is an excellent source of up to date information. Legal periodicals such as the *Law Society Gazette* and the *Solicitors Journal* also weigh in with informative articles on media law matters, particularly defamation. Media periodicals such as the *Press Gazette* and the Press Association's *Media Lawyer* are also excellent sources of information but often looked at through media coloured spectacles.

Tutors will have a pecking order of the importance they attach to these sources. Generally, there will be an assumption that it is preferable to quote from or refer to established journals that attract comment from serious academics. I wouldn't seek to dissuade you from using these sources, but, with this subject, they may have limited appeal simply because things change so quickly. Your course could have finished before a detailed article on an important point of media law appears in one of these journals! This is where the newspapers and weekly periodicals can prove very useful.

The Press Gazette's comments on legal matters will usually come from practising media lawyers and should therefore be regarded as influential. Another really good source of up-to-date comment that can be used for revision purposes is the websites of barristers' chambers or solicitors' practices. The following are very helpful as they deal with current case issues:

- www.onebrickcourt.com
- www.5rb.co.uk
- www.carter-ruck.com

- *Manage your time well. That applies throughout the year, not just at revision time.*
- *Don't let your work build up throughout the year. Identify major issues as you go along.*
- *Don't try to keep absorbing more and more facts – revise constructively in the sense of noting criticism and analysis of the case law.*
- *Set yourself a day-by-day timetable and try to stick to it.*
- *Use past examination papers as a guide to future papers. The topics rarely change but the issues will. The structure of questions will also remain pretty consistent.*
- *Always know why you are revising a particular topic. It will relate to the issues that you think may arise. So, ask yourself before you begin, 'What are the issues connected with …?'*

How you do your revision will, of course, depend on your own motivation. Do think about revision throughout the year and prepare for it as you go along. After each topic has been discussed, it should help if you make a summary note of the legal issues that have been identified. Those summary notes can then form the basis of your revision strategy. In fact, if you prepare these summary notes throughout the year, you don't even have to wait for revision time to utilise them – they can be read anywhere at your convenience.

Academic success has much to do with good organisation and planning. The value of the material that you have accumulated over the year may well be diminished if you do not organise it into an easily retrievable form.

As I mentioned above, you should make use of past examination papers. Below, I will give you an example of a question from an examination paper and suggest how best to answer it in a way that should meet an examiner's expectations. You should never confine revision to memory work and then hope that you can regurgitate it in a coherent and appropriate fashion in the examination. It will rarely, if ever, work to your advantage. Therefore, the combination of looking at past examination papers and the key features of each topic that you have identified should help to make revision a comfortable and reassuring experience.

In the process of revision, take care not to become a hermit. Revision need not be a solitary experience. Do discuss past questions with your friends. See whether their interpretation of a question is the same as yours. In this way, you should be able to gain further reassurance that you are working along the right lines. If all else fails, talk to or e-mail your tutor. After all, it is a key part of our role to give academic support to our students.

Are you one of those students who thrives on mnemonics – devices that will help you recall information that might otherwise be difficult to retrieve from your memory? If so, with media law, you might want to relate legal principles to celebrities. So, *Campbell* links to privacy and confidentiality, *Galloway* links to common law qualified privilege, *Branson* links to fair comment and so on.

Acronyms, too, can be useful. Simply take the first letters of key words and make a new word from them. The trouble with this system is that the more words you create, the more chance there is of confusion! If it helps you, fine, but if not, don't bother trying.

Finally, take a break from revision when you feel it is necessary. There is no point trying to revise if your mind is elsewhere. The writer's block syndrome can affect revision as well. You might timetable breaks into your revision schedule, but I think that can be counterproductive. If, like me, you take a while to get started, the last thing you need to do is take a break simply because your timetable says, '11 a.m. break for 30 minutes.' Keep going for as long as you feel the effort is paying dividends, *then* take a break. That break may be longer than you envisaged, but it doesn't matter too much, providing your overall time management is good. Restart when you feel in the mood. An hour of productive working is better than 3 hours of stop/start revision when your concentration is lapsing.

3.7	
examination hints and tips	

The most obvious piece of information, but the most important, is to ascertain exactly *when* your examinations are, at which *venue* and the *time* they commence. Little can be done to help you if you miss an examination, other than to prepare yourself for taking the examination at resit time instead!

It is not unusual to be nervous prior to an examination. If you have undertaken thorough revision then you should not be unduly worried. Examinations are designed to be fair tests of what you have studied. They are not designed to trip you up. Keep thinking positively and do not listen to others outside the examination room because they are bound to mention something that you considered unimportant or have not read. If it is going to be important there is not a lot you can do at this stage to remedy the problem, so keep focused on what you *do* know rather than on what you *don't*.

Keep that focus on the major topics that you have prepared to answer questions about. Go over the major points of the key cases in your mind. Resolve to write certain things down as soon as the examination starts because it is all too easy to find that something cannot be recalled instantly in the heat of the moment. Read all the questions and just jot the names of the important cases down for each one prior to starting the examination, particularly in relation to the question you are likely to answer last, when you will probably be under some time pressure.

Once in the examination hall, time management becomes very important. First, check the rubric on the examination paper to confirm what you already believed you knew. Do you really have to answer three questions in two hours or is it two questions in three hours? Are any of the questions compulsory? It is a good idea not to leave a compulsory question to last. Attempt it first because it is likely to be on a topic that your tutors have told you is important and therefore you have given it a reasonable amount of revision time in the expectation that it would appear. Sometimes your tutors will tell you what the topic of the compulsory question is going to be.

Look carefully to see if the paper is in sections and whether or not you have to attempt a question from each section and, say, one other from any section. Are there sections on the paper that don't apply to your particular option group? Please believe me when I say that I have had postgraduate students who have apparently been unable to comprehend simple instructions and confine themselves to the correct sections of the paper.

Once you know what to do, the next decision for you to make is which questions to answer. Try to read the questions as carefully as possible, bearing in mind exactly what the question asks you to do. Are you expected to 'analyse' or 'apply' or 'critically consider' or 'describe'? The question for you to answer before choosing a question is 'Do I have enough knowledge to answer this question well?' Note that this does not mean 'Do I know enough about the broad topic to regurgitate information on it?' but, 'Can I apply my knowledge to the problem question in front of me?'

Once you have made the selection, decide which questions to prioritise. This may be done purely on the basis of your knowledge of the subject matter or you may do this on the basis of the number of marks to be awarded for each question or part of a question. In practice, you will usually choose on the basis of knowledge and attempt your 'best' question first. Never forget the basic rule that every answer should have an introduction, middle (with subconclusions) and an overall conclusion. Do state in the introduction what you believe the question is asking you to do.

For example, the following is a question from a 2006 examination paper:

David is a reporter for a Sunday tabloid called The Revelation. *Tom, the manager of the EYE, a celebrity nightclub in the centre of Manchester, is David's friend. Tom tells David that the club's CCTV security cameras often contain, as he puts it, 'X-rated' action when couples are caught engaging in 'heavy petting' sessions, often fuelled by drink. Seeing the potential, David offers Tom £1,000 for a copy of any CCTV footage containing indiscreet behaviour by well-known celebrities.*

Two weeks ago, Tom delivered a videotape that showed Lottie, a famous pop singer, and her current boyfriend engaging in sexual behaviour. The video showed the time to be 3 a.m. and the location of the 'action' was in a secluded corner of the club well away from the bar and dance floor. The newspaper paid Tom £1,000 for the video. However, unknown to David, Tom had already made six copies of the tape and was intent on selling them to an Internet service provider.

Last Sunday, The Revelation *published a number of stills from the video as a 'taster' for more explicit photographs the next week. Lottie's lawyer has now written to the newspaper informing the Editor that Lottie will be seeking an injunction to prevent stills from the video being published and damages for the breach of her privacy as a result of the initial publication.*

Critically consider the legal implications arising from these facts.

A first analysis of this question would probably lead you to make brief notes like the following.

- legal context: privacy and confidentiality
- prior restraint: injunctions
- damages for what has been published – is this a breach of privacy/confidentiality?
- copyright issues
- elements of the law to rely on
- defences for newspaper: Press Complaints Commission Code of Practice
- action against whom – newspaper and/or Tom?
- cases: *McKennitt, Charles, Ashley Cole, Jagger, Theakston, Caroline, Campbell, A v. B & C. J. Douglas.*

So your introductory paragraph could look something like this:

This question requires us to critically consider the legal implications arising from the above facts. The major legal topics for discussion would appear to centre on the law relating to confidentiality and privacy. There is also a secondary issue connected with potential copyright infringement. Finally, an examination of the legal issues must conclude with an assessment of any remedies available to Lottie, including an assessment of the law on prior restraint and its relationship to freedom of expression.

You would then go on to commence the critical analysis part of the answer. One way to do this would be to take an 'issues' approach. Ask yourself, 'What is the first event or issue about which Lottie feels aggrieved?' The stills have been published, so you might begin with a discussion centred on whether or not she can obtain damages for the publication of the stills and against whom the remedy would lie. The contenders are, of course, the newspaper and Tom. This, in turn, will permit you to discuss whether or not there has been a breach of confidentiality or privacy and to consider the impact of the current case law, including the European Court of Human Rights' decision in the *Caroline* case. At the heart of the discussion will be whether or not Lottie had *a reasonable expectation of privacy* in the club at that time in the morning. This will allow you to take into account the reasoning in the *Jagger* case and to contrast it with the High Court's decision in the *Theakston* case. You will then need to assess the importance of the case law developments in the last 12 months, including *McKennitt* and the *HRH the Prince of Wales* decisions.

Once you have done this to your satisfaction, then you can write your subconclusion and move on to the next element of the question.

That is likely to be the question of *injunctions*. Clearly, pictures have been published, but it is alleged that more explicit photographs will appear the following week. Should this be prevented? After all, Article 10 is in favour of freedom of expression and we do live in a democracy with a free press! Conversely, the publication of the photographs will cause acute embarrassment to Lottie, but should not necessarily have an adverse effect on her career.

This will lead into a discussion on the relative merits of Article 8 against Article 10 and how a court might resolve the conflict. There is also the matter of the law on prior restraint (mention *Cream Holdings*) and that is very much in favour of freedom of expression, with any potential remedies coming ex post facto. This section will then be ended by a subconclusion.

You can then move on to discuss the *copyright* implications. You are not told whether or not the newspaper has bought the copyright, only that it has bought a videotape of the images contained on it. Equally, Tom, who is only the manager of the club, will, in all probability, have no legal rights to the ownership of the video. Injunctions could be sought against the owner of the club, although you are not told of his or her intentions regarding the tape's contents.

Finally, you would write your overall conclusion. Usually examiners will not be too concerned if your conclusions don't match theirs, so long as you have argued authoritatively, using appropriate source material.

Prior to starting to write, decide how much time you will allocate to each question. Undergraduate examination papers usually demand answers to four questions in three hours or three in two and a half hours. It is crucial that you do not spend too much time on your earlier answers, leaving too little time for the final answer. Failure to plan your time properly can mean the difference between an upper and lower second classification. All the good work of, say, two questions can be undone by a poor third answer. Let me illustrate this point.

Assume that you have to answer three questions. The first answer is good and given a mark of 65 per cent. Your second answer is also pretty good and given a mark of 60 per cent. So far, you are heading for a 2.1. Now, let us assume that, because of poor time management, you do not complete the third answer and are awarded a 'generous' 49 per cent. Your total mark is 174/300. The average mark is now 58 per cent. In other words, you are 2 per cent below the 2.1 standard. 'Aha'! you may say, 'but I have two marks in the upper category.' That may be true, but one examination board convention is that the upper and lower marks (the 65 and 49) cancel each other out, giving an average of 57 per cent. In effect, your marks are 57, 57 and 60 per cent. An examination board is likely to conclude that there is no overall evidence of a 2.1 standard. It will be clear that this situation has arisen because of the poor third answer. Let me assure you, this is not a contrived example. Having been an external examiner at a number of UK universities, I have, on many occasions, seen students I thought had demonstrated that they were of a 2:1 standard fail to achieve it because they had let themselves down by having a third class mark, simply due to poor time management. It's a simple proposition, but one cannot award high marks for what isn't there.

3.8	
good luck	

I hope that you will be interested and motivated by the study of media law. It is a subject that invariably contains much that is current and to which you can relate. Members of the general public seem to be avid readers of both newspapers and magazines. It is claimed there are some 20,000 magazine titles in the UK alone! Everything about the law that applies to newspapers also applies to magazines.

If you take on board the points that I have raised in this part of the book, you can look forward to achieving high grades in your assessment. It is now down to you to prove to yourself and others that you can grasp the nettle and succeed.

part four
case notes

- Introduction
- European case law
- Case law from the USA
- English case law
- Contempt of court: prejudicial reporting

4.1

introduction

These case notes are meant to assist you in understanding the material in this book, without the necessity of having a law report in front of you. However, they are not designed to be a substitute for actually reading the cases in the law reports or major textbooks for yourself. It is hoped that they will also act as a useful revision aid.

Note that the cases are in alphabetical order within each section.

4.2

european case law

Murphy v. Ireland [2003] ECHR 352

The Irish Faith Centre submitted an advertisement to an independent commercial radio station. It read:

> *What think ye of Christ? Would you, like Peter, only say that he is the son of the living God? Have you ever exposed yourself to the historical facts about Christ? The Irish Faith Centre are presenting for Easter week an hour long video ... on the evidence of the resurrection from Monday 10th–Saturday 15th April every night at 8:30 and Easter Sunday at 11:30 a.m. and also live by satellite at 7.30 p.m.*

The Independent Radio and Television Commission stopped the broadcast under section 10(3) of the Radio and Television Act 1988. It stated:

> *No advertisement shall be broadcast which is directed towards any religious or political end or which has any relation to an industrial dispute.*

Held

Article 10 rights had not been violated because the applicant could have used many other means to disseminate the information, particularly through the print media.

Factors to note

- Subsequent legislation – the Broadcasting Act 2001 – amended section 10(3) to permit broadcasting that states religious magazines or newspapers are for sale or advertising a religious event or a ceremony. However, this did not make any difference to this case as the advertisement had been placed in 1995.
- Note the 'margin of appreciation', which is allowed to governments by the European Court. A reduced 'margin of appreciation' applied when the advertisement prohibited concerned a matter of public interest.
- The 'margin of appreciation' is relevant when assessing the compatibility of a legislative provision with the Convention.
- Other factors would include whether or not the interference corresponded with a 'pressing social need' and if it was 'proportionate to the legitimate aim pursued'.
- Another concern for the court was the relative financial strength of the organisation placing the advertisement. It was felt that there might be a link or association between a deep purse and overbearing religious broadcasting.
- The court believed the audio-visual media to be more 'powerful' than the print media.

Selistö v. Finland [2004] ECHR 634

The applicant was a journalist living and working in Finland. In two articles in 1996, she described the allegedly unprofessional behaviour of a surgeon, which, it was claimed, had led to his patient's death. The police and the National Medico-Legal Board carried out investigations into the death, but no causal connection between the surgeon's conduct and the consequence could be established. The surgeon in question alleged that the articles were defamatory in that they alleged he had committed a criminal offence and, as a result, the public prosecutor brought proceedings against the journalist under the Finnish Penal Code. She was convicted of defamation committed 'despite better knowledge.' In broad terms, the Code seeks to penalise journalists who fail to carry out adequate research or engage in irresponsible journalism that results in a person being wrongly accused of committing an offence.

The journalist brought the case to the European Court of Human rights on the basis that her conviction for such an offence was contrary to her Article 10 rights of freedom of expression. The Court noted that it was 'common ground' between the parties that the applicant's conviction constituted an interference with her right to freedom of expression under Article 10(1). It was also agreed that the interference was prescribed by law and pursued a legitimate aim, namely the protection of reputation or rights of others within the meaning of Article 10(2).

The only dispute related to the question of whether or not the interference was 'necessary in a democratic society.'

Held

In order to decide if the 'necessity' of the restriction had been established convincingly, it had to be asked whether or not the applicant's conviction struck a *fair balance* between the public interests involved and the interests of the surgeon.

The court found that the issues raised by the journalist were 'important matters of public concern' and, therefore, outweighed the 'undoubted interests of X in protecting his professional reputation.' The reasons relied on by the state were deemed insufficient to show that the interference complained of was 'necessary in a democratic' society.

Accordingly, there had been a violation of Article 10 of the Convention. However, please note that the decision was 6:1 and you would be well advised to read and note the reasoning of Sir Nicolas Bratza, the British judge, who believed that, in order to gain the protection of Article 10, a journalist must act *responsibly*. The factors that had weighed heavily with the majority were:

- it had not been claimed that the actual facts were erroneous
- despite the reporting being 'somewhat one-sided' it had been based on information included in pre-trial reports
- in 2001, the Deputy Parliamentary Ombudsman found that it would have been preferable if charges had been brought against X
- X's name or other personal details including his sex were not mentioned
- X was provided with the opportunity to comment after each article.

In Sir Nicolas' view, 'none of these factors, whether considered individually or cumulatively, are such as to justify the conclusion that the domestic courts exceeded any acceptable margin of appreciation.' You may feel that there are overtones of the *Reynolds* reasoning in the minority opinion and, in particular, Lord Nicholls' ten factors of responsible journalism (see case note for *Reynolds v. Times Newspapers* where each factor is described).

VgT Verein Gegen Tierfabriken v. Switzerland [2001] ECHR 412

VgT Verein Gegen Tierfabriken is an association that exist to campaign for the protection of animals, with the emphasis on preventing animal experimentation and industrial animal production.

As a reaction to various television commercials promoted by the Swiss meat industry, the association prepared a television commercial lasting 55 seconds and consisting of 2 scenes. The first showed a sow building a shelter in the forest for her piglets and was accompanied by soft background music. The second showed a noisy hall with pigs in small pens gnawing nervously at the iron bars. The voiceover drew comparisons with concentration camps. The commercial ended with the exhortation, 'Eat less meat, for the sake of your health, the animals and the environment.'

Before the commercial could be broadcast, it had to be vetted by the commercial television company and permission was refused on the grounds that the content was of a 'clear political character'. Suggestions were offered to the association on how the video could comply with the decision, but the association refused to compromise. The ban on political advertising is contained in section 18(5) of the Federal Radio and Television Law 1991. One purpose of this legislation is to prevent 'financially powerful groups from obtaining competitive political advantage. Public opinion should not be influenced by "undue commercial pressure"'.

Under the Law, religious and political advertising is prohibited.

The key question was whether or not the refusal to broadcast the commercial fell within Article 10(2). The right to exercise freedom of expression under Article 10(1) may be subject to such *'formalities, conditions, restrictions or penalties as are prescribed by law and are necessary in a democratic society ...'* (Article 10(2)).

Held

The court found that this type of advertising fell outside the usual type of advertisement, exhorting people to buy things. It reflected 'controversial opinions pertaining to modern society in general.' The court also considered the proportionality of the measure vis-à-vis the aim pursued.

The court concluded that the association's Article 10 rights had been violated. It pointed out that the restriction applied only to radio and television and concluded that a prohibition on political advertising only applying to certain media did not appear to be of a pressing nature. Therefore, in finding for the applicant, the court concluded that the measure could not be considered 'necessary in a democratic society.'

<table>
<tr><td>

4.3

case law from the USA

</td><td>

</td></tr>
</table>

New York Times v. Sullivan [1964] 376 US 254

In March 1960, *The New York Times* carried an advertisement entitled 'Heed Their Rising Voices'. It was designed to persuade people to help fund the civil rights campaigns in the southern states. The advertisement went into some detail about alleged civil rights abuses and was critical of the police in Montgomery, Alabama.

It was admitted that some of the material was inaccurate and the Police Commissioner brought an action for libel, even though he was not named in the advertisement. Local law prevented such an action being brought by public officials unless they had first requested a public retraction. *The New York Times* refused. Commissioner Sullivan won $500,000 in damages from an Alabama jury.

Decision of the Supreme Court

The rule of law, as applied by the Alabama courts, was deemed constitutionally inadequate because of its failure to provide safeguards for freedom of speech and the press, as demanded by the 1st and 14th amendments to the Constitution of the USA. The lack of proper safeguards meant that the evidence presented could not support the judgment of the state court.

<table>
<tr><td>

4.4

english case law

</td><td>

</td></tr>
</table>

A v. B & C [2002] EWCA Civ 337

A Premiership footballer had, over a lengthy period, engaged in adulterous relations with two women – one described as a nursery school teacher, the other a lap dancer. *The People* newspaper wanted to publish their stories.

The footballer sought an injunction to prevent the stories becoming public on the grounds of breach of confidence and breach of privacy.

The trial judge decided that an injunction should be granted. The judge acknowledged that details of sexual relations within marriage are protected by the law of confidentiality. The question was whether or not sexual relations outside of marriage and in the absence of any express agreement should be covered by the same law. The judge took the view that the footballer had not courted publicity and, in the context of 'modern sexual relations', ought to be able to prevent publication. The newspaper appealed.

Held

The injunction was lifted. The court recognised that such an action was an unjustified interference in freedom of expression.

The case is interesting for the Lord Chief Justice's attempt to establish guidelines for judges when dealing with applications for interim injunctions based on breach of confidence. The guidelines, however, go further than mere procedural matters and embrace matters of substantive law. These must be treated with some care, given the decision in *Cream Holdings [2004] HL*. Nevertheless, the case was cited with approval by the Court of Appeal in *Jameel v. Wall Street Journal Europe [2005]*, to confirm that the 'public interest' does not necessarily coincide with what might be regarded as 'of interest to the public'. You might be forgiven for believing that the proposition was not in doubt, except Lord Woolf went further, seeming to associate himself with the proposition that newspapers should be led in their decision making by what interests the public, 'otherwise there will be fewer newspapers published, which will not be in the public interest.'

There are 15 'guidelines'. Be aware of them, but also recognise that the law on confidentiality, privacy and prior restraint has moved rapidly since this decision (see *Campbell [2004]*, *Von Hannover [2004]*, *Cream Holdings [2004]*, *Greene v. Associated Newspapers [2004]*, *McKennitt v. Ash [2005]* and *Prince Charles [2006]*).

Ackroyd v. Mersey Care Health Trust [2003] EWCA Civ 663

Having been identified as the intermediary in the *Ashworth* case, the Trust sought an order to force Ackroyd to disclose the name of the informant inside Ashworth Hospital. In the first instance, Gray J ordered him to release the name of his source.

Held (allowing the appeal)

On appeal, it was judged that Ackroyd should *not* be forced to name the informant because of the following points.

- He had an arguable defence based on the public interest once it had become clear that his source had not been motivated to release the information by financial considerations.
- Time had passed and there had been no further breaches of confidentiality in respect of clinical records. The impact of the House of Lords' decision was well known: 'The vital principle as to the confidentiality of medical records has been established unequivocally by the House of Lords' decision, and employees who breach that principle in the future can be in no doubt of the risks that they incur' (Carnwath LJ). Therefore there was no 'pressing need' to order the release of the informant's name.

(See also below, *Mersey Care NHS Trust v. Ackroyd [2006] EWHC 107 (QB)*

Armstrong v. Times Newspapers [2004] EWHC 2928 (QB)

This case was decided one month after the *Galloway v. Telegraph Group [2004]* case by the same judge, Eady J. Once again, when assessing the defence of qualified privilege he considered each of Reynolds' 'ten non-exhaustive criteria' before concluding that *The Sunday Times* could not rely on the defence of qualified privilege. The judge decided that the newspaper could not be said to be under a duty to publish allegations to the effect that Armstrong had *probably* taken performance-enhancing drugs or, given his success in the Tour de France, that he 'must' have done so. The judge also held that, before publishing, he should have been given an opportunity to make a 'measured response' to the charges. In other words, once again, a newspaper had failed to apply the basic requirements needed to qualify as responsible journalism and thereby warrant the protection of common law qualified privilege.

However, the Court of Appeal in *Armstrong v. Times Newspapers Ltd & Others [2005] EWCA Civ 1007* had to answer the question of whether or not the *Reynolds* defence had been legitimately denied to the newspaper, given that it had been summarily dismissed under the Civil Procedure Rules at a preliminary stage.

Held

It was held that the issue should not have been disposed of at this stage and the matter of privilege should be tested at trial. Do note, however, that the court was not saying that the *approach* to *Reynolds* privilege adopted by the judge at first instance was wrong. Whether or not the *Reynolds* privilege defence was *appropriate* was a matter for the trial.

Ashworth Hospital Authority v. MGN Ltd [2002] UKHL 29

Ashworth Hospital houses some of the most dangerous people in the UK. One of its patients is Ian Brady, sentenced to life imprisonment at Chester Assizes in 1966 for murder in what became known as the Moors Murders.

In 1999, he went on hunger strike in protest at alleged mistreatment from an alleged unprovoked attack by a number of warders in riot gear. There were also serious allegations made relating to the mismanagement of the hospital that resulted in an official inquiry. An employee at the hospital released clinical notes relating to Brady to Robin Ackroyd, an investigative journalist, who sold them to the *Daily Mirror*. They were subsequently used in an article relating to conditions at the hospital. The hospital wanted to identify the source of the leaked information and sought an order from the courts.

Held (HL)

The *Daily Mirror* was ordered to release the name of the intermediary (Ackroyd). The House acknowledged the importance of privacy when it came to dealing with patient's records or clinical notes. The House believed that disclosure of the employee was necessary in order to deter similar wrongdoing in the future. It acknowledged that running a secure hospital of this type was 'fraught with difficulty and danger' and concluded that the disclosure of patients' records 'increases that difficulty and danger.' It was that, said Lord Woolf, which 'made the orders to disclose necessary and proportionate and justified.' The court also considered the relationship between Articles 8 and 10 of the European Convention and that protection of medical data was of fundamental importance to a person's enjoyment of his or her right to respect for private and family life.

Attorney General v. Associated Newspapers [1994] 1 All ER 556

The *Mail on Sunday* published an article in which it revealed the content of deliberations by some members of the jury at a highly publicised fraud trial. Some jurors had given the information to a third party, believing that they were taking part in bona fide research. The newspaper had obtained the information from these transcripts, not directly from jury members. Contempt proceedings for breach of section 8(1) of the Contempt of Court Act 1981 were brought by the Attorney General.

Held (HL)

It was contempt for a newspaper to publish such information, even though it was obtained from a third party. The House considered section 8(1) to be 'plain and unambiguous'. What had happened amounted to a 'disclosure' in the context of section 8. The newspaper was fined £30,000, the editor £20,000 and the journalist responsible for the article £10,000.

Attorney General v. English [1983] 1 AC 116 [1982] 2 All ER 903

A well-known paediatrician had been accused of murdering a Down's Syndrome baby. *The Daily Mail* published an article by Malcolm Muggeridge during the course of the trial, ostensibly in support of a pro-life candidate at a forthcoming election. The article referred to the 'fact' that it was 'common practice amongst paediatricians to let severely physically and mentally handicapped babies die of starvation'. The Attorney General brought contempt proceedings against the newspaper.

Held (HL)

The section 5 defence succeeded. The article did not make specific reference to the trial and the House felt that, as the pro-life candidate was seeking election on the basis that this type of behaviour did occur, then *not* to refer to it would have made the article meaningless.

Examiners would appreciate seeing a reference to the following quotation from Lord Diplock (at p. 920) as to the purpose of section 5:

> [The gagging of bona fide public discussion in the press of controversial matters of general public interest, merely because there are in existence contemporaneous legal proceedings in which some particular instance of those controversial matters may be in issue, is what s.5 of the Contempt of Court Act 1981 was in my view intended to prevent.

Branson v. Bower [2001] EWCA Civ 791

Bower wrote an article for the *Evening Standard* in December 1999 at the time of the launch of Sir Richard Branson's second attempt to obtain a National Lottery licence. Branson complained of two innuendoes he claimed asserted that he was a hypocrite and was organising his bid for the lottery franchise not for charitable motives but out of revenge and self-interest and as a means of gaining free publicity for the Virgin brand. One passage read 'Revenge rather than pure self-righteousness has motivated Richard Branson's latest bid to run Britain's Lottery ... sceptics will inevitably whisper that Branson's motive is self glorification'.

Held (CA)

The Court of Appeal, having read the article as a whole, found that the trial judge was entitled to conclude that the respondent was:

> *expressing a series of opinions about the motives of the appellant in a way that would have left the reader in no doubt that they were inferences drawn by the respondent from the facts set out in the article.*

Bunt v. Tilley [2006] EWHC 407 (QB)

The claimant took exception to postings made on internet chat rooms, considering them defamatory of him. He took action against the individuals concerned and also brought proceedings against their internet service providers. In the claimant's opinion the ISP's had provided the means for the individuals to post the allegedly defamatory material on the net. The questions for the court were whether the ISP's were 'publishers' under common law and whether they had defences based on section 1 of the Defamation Act 1996 or the Electronic Commerce (EC Directive) Regulations 2002.

Held

The court regarded each ISP as a 'passive' medium of communication similar to a telephone company and as such there would be no liability at common law. The assumption was that the ISP's, while facilitating the communications, would be unaware that these allegedly defamatory postings had been made. The case is therefore distinguished from that of *Godfrey v. Demon Internet* because the ISP's in this case had not received notice of the existence of the postings. Second, the court granted the ISP's protection under the Directive, regarding them as a 'mere conduit' under Regulation 17, which provided an appropriate defence.

To fully appreciate the impact of this decision please look at section 1 of the Defamation Act 1996 and the Electronic Commerce Regulations 2002.

Camelot v. Centaur Communications Ltd [1997] EWCA Civ 2554

This case gets a passing mention because it was the first English case to take into account the European Court's decision in *Goodwin*. The Court of Appeal took the view that, while the *conclusions* of the House of Lords and the European Court based on the facts may have been different, the *approaches* adopted were similar – that is, appropriate weight was given to Article 10 rights. At the time Camelot was (and still is) the company authorised to run the National Lottery. Draft accounts were leaked to a magazine and the contents published, causing much embarrassment to the company and, incidentally, to the government. The article contended that the salaries of directors had increased while money for charitable purposes had declined.

The company wished to have the documents supplied by an unknown source returned in the hope of identifying that person. An injunction was obtained preventing further disclosures and an assurance given that nothing more would be published that didn't appear in the full audited accounts.

Held (CA)

The Court ordered that the documents should be returned. It was stated that the law does not enable the press to protect anonymity in *all* circumstances. The trial judge concluded that the public interest in enabling the plaintiff to discover the identity of a disloyal employee was greater than in enabling him to escape detection. The court alluded to the European Court's words to the effect that companies often 'had a legitimate reason as a commercial enterprise in unmasking a disloyal employee or collaborator who might have continuing access to its premises in order to terminate his or her association with the company.'

Campbell v. MGN Ltd [2004] UKHL 22

The supermodel Naomi Campbell was featured in an article in the *Daily Mirror* about her drug habit. It was illustrated by a photograph of her coming out of a meeting of Narcotics Anonymous. The photograph was taken without her knowledge or consent. The rather sympathetic story by the newspaper sought to correct the impression she had given previously that, unlike other supermodels, she did not take drugs. Her response was to take an action initially based on breach of confidence and invasion of privacy. The latter cause of action was subsequently dropped.

Held

The trial judge found in her favour. The court applied the three major criteria for establishing confidence laid down in the *Coco* case. The *Daily Mirror,* not surprisingly, attempted to argue that public interest should override any apparent breach of confidence.

The *Daily Mirror* appealed to the Court of Appeal and won. The newspaper was entitled to correct the record regarding her drugtaking and it was considered legitimate to illustrate the story with the photograph of her exiting from Narcotics Anonymous. The whole thing should be regarded as one package.

However, this was not the view of the House of Lords, where, by a 3:2 majority, her appeal was allowed. The minority based their decision on freedom of expression and the fact that the photograph was complementary to the article about her drugtaking. However, the majority took a 'personal' approach and felt that the photograph in particular was intrusive and, if photographers were to be further permitted to photograph her in these circumstances, she might deny herself the treatment she sought.

The House spurned the opportunity that many had expected them to take, which was to rule on whether or not English law should establish a tort of privacy.

Charleston v. News Group Newspapers [1995] 2 All ER 313

The *News of the World* published photographs in which the heads of a well-known actor and actress were superimposed on the bodies of two people engaged in various sexual activities. On the same page, there was a photograph in which the first plaintiff's head was superimposed on a woman dressed in a skintight leather outfit that exposed her breasts. A banner headline read:

STREWTH! WHAT'S HAROLD UP TO WITH OUR MADGE?

Below was a smaller, but still prominent, secondary headline that read

Porn shocker for Neighbour's stars

The accompanying article made it clear that the images had been produced as part of a pornographic computer game and the plaintiff's face had been used without her knowledge or consent and described her and her co-star as 'victims'.

The plaintiffs sued for libel, claiming that the *ordinary* and *natural* meaning was that they had posed for pornographic photographs.

The judge at first instance and the Court of Appeal held that the publications were not capable of bearing the meanings pleaded.

Held

On appeal to the House of Lords, the appeal was dismissed. A prominent headline or headline and photograph could *not* found a claim for libel *in isolation* from the related test of an accompanying article that was not defamatory when considered as a whole. In this case, parts of the article negated any effect of the libel perpetrated by the photographs and headlines. The House was aware that there would be a limited number of people who, for whatever reason, would see only the headlines or the photographs and would not read the text. However, the court was not prepared to assess the impact on that limited group of people – it was that which was conveyed to ordinary, reasonable, fair-minded readers that mattered.

The trainee journalists among you will probably be aware that, in order to succeed with the *bane and antidote* defence, the 'antidote' should be situated close to the 'bane' on the page, otherwise reasonable readers may not make the connection between the two.

Clayton v Clayton [2006] EWCA 878

I have included reference to this case, decided in June 2006, because of the ongoing discussions currently taking place at government level about introducing greater transparency into the Family Court system. For further information on the wider issues of transparency, please see the Department of Constitutional Affairs website at www.dca.gov.uk and access the Consultation Report by typing in 'Confidence/Confidentially. Improving Transparency and Privacy in the Family Courts.'

The following summary of the *Clayton* decision is to be found at page 24 of the Consultation Report:

> The case clarifies that criminal sanctions for publishing material identifying a child involved in any proceedings only last while the proceedings are current. However, contempt of court provisions continue to apply and the court also retains its power to make specific orders about the child and any media activity. When deciding whether to make such an order the court will balance the child's right to privacy against any competing right to freedom of expression under the ECHR.

Brief facts

The custody dispute between the parents was settled in 2005. The father was a father's rights campaigner and wished to discuss elements of the case with the media. However, at the conclusion of the proceedings the judge, purporting to act in the child's best interests had made an order preventing public debate on the case. The judge, in effect, interpreted section 97 of the Children Act 1989 as authority preventing naming the child until its 18th birthday had been reached.

Held

The section only prevented publication of identifying information until the conclusion of the proceedings. Therefore at the conclusion of such proceedings, consideration should take place as to whether the reporting of the case should be prohibited in order to prevent identification of the child. Clearly Articles 8 and 10 rights are to be taken into account as well as the age of the child and the circumstances of the case. From a media perspective it must not be automatically assumed that reporting is prohibited (consider this case when reading pages 89–91 dealing with children in civil proceedings).

Cream Holdings Ltd & Others v. Banerjee & Others
[2004] UKHL 44

Cream Holdings was a group of companies operating nightclubs, initially in Liverpool and then elsewhere in the country. Banerjee was a financial controller for one of the Cream companies. She was dismissed in 2001 and took with her, without permission, documents belonging to Cream Holdings that, she claimed, showed illegal and improper activity by the Cream group. One allegation related to corruption involving a director of the company and a local council official. She took the documents to the *Liverpool Echo*. Cream sought injunctive relief to prevent the newspaper from publishing confidential information that had been, it claimed, improperly obtained.

Held (HL)

The House had no doubts that the story was of serious public concern and interest. It involved allegations of corruption and it was the newspapers' job as public 'watchdogs' to bring such matters to public attention. The court had to consider the meaning of section 12(3) of the Human Rights Act 1998. This states that no relief which might affect the Convention right of freedom of expression is to be granted so as to restrain publication before trial *unless* the court is satisfied that the applicant is likely to establish that publication should not be allowed.

The House referred to this as the 'threshold test'. In considering the meaning of the word 'likely', the House concluded that it meant 'a likelihood of success at the trial higher than [a] "real prospect" but permitting the court to dispense with this higher standard where particular circumstances make this necessary.'

There could be no single rigid standard governing all applications for interim restraint orders. The following two major points emerge:

- A court will not make an interim restraint order unless it is satisfied that the applicant's prospects of success at the trial 'are sufficiently favourable to justify such an order being made in the particular circumstances of the case.'
- Courts will be 'exceedingly slow to make interim restraint orders when the applicant has not satisfied the court he will probably (more likely than not) succeed at the trial. In general that must be the *threshold* an applicant must cross before the court embarks on exercising judicial discretion.'

The application for an injunction was refused.

Douglas v. Hello! Ltd [2003] EWHC 786 (CH)

The film stars Michael Douglas and Catherine Zeta-Jones sold, for £1 million, exclusive rights to *OK* magazine to publish their wedding photographs. The wedding took place at the Plaza Hotel in New York, the happy couple having taken over a whole floor of the hotel. Elaborate security precautions had been taken to ensure that guests did not bring cameras to the event. Nevertheless, photographs, albeit of poor quality, were taken and eventually sold to *Hello!*, *OK's* rival magazine, and subsequently published.

The couple, together with *OK*, sued *Hello!* for breach of confidence and invasion of privacy.

Held

The action succeeded, but only on the basis of breach of confidence. The court acknowledged that the Douglases had 'a claim to personal confidence weakened by sale and the intention to publish', but, nevertheless, that did not change the fact that *Hello!* had sought, unconscionably 'to anticipate that publication.'

The judge then turned his attention to privacy and refused to hold that there was an existing law of privacy under which the 'claimants ... are entitled to relief.' He believed that, even if there had been a law of privacy, the claimants would not have been able to make 'any recovery greater than that which is open to them under the law of confidence'.

In summary, the reasons given for not recognising a tort of privacy in the case were that:

- higher judicial support for such a law had been confined to comments by Sedley LJ in the Court of Appeal judgment in this case in 2000 when the Douglases first sought an injunction to prevent the photographs from being published and other members of the court did not endorse his opinion
- the Douglases could bring their case within the law of confidence, so this proved that English law was not inadequate when it came to providing remedies for this type of breach of 'privacy'
- Parliament should legislate because that would result in a more coherent law than if judges were to decide on a case-by-case basis
- Lindsay J cited Lord Woolf's view in *A v. B & C [2002]* that the law on confidence would provide adequate remedies in most 'privacy' actions
- the damages awarded were likely to be the same, whether the action was founded on breach of privacy or confidence.

(See now the Court of Appeal's decision in *Douglas v. Hello! Ltd [2005] EWCA Civ 595*, where the 'privacy' award was upheld by the court. It was also asserted by the Master of the Rolls that breach of confidence was the appropriate remedy, despite the comment that privacy situations were having to be 'shoehorned' into the existing cause of action for breach of confidence.)

Dow Jones & Co Inc. v. Jameel [2005] EWCA Civ 75

In March 2003, the defendants placed an article on its website, which was hosted in New Jersey. The offending article remained on the site for some four months before being removed.

The claimant alleged that the article said he had been, or was suspected of having been, involved in funding al-Qaeda. The website was accessible to subscribers around the world, including 6,000 in the UK.

The defendants believed that no more than five subscribers actually accessed the article. In consequence, they claimed that it was an abuse of process to permit the action for defamation to proceed.

Held

The Court of Appeal allowed the appeal. It confirmed the 'established and irrebuttable presumption' in defamation law, which is that the claimant having suffered damage is not incompatible with freedom of expression. The court went on to state that, in maintaining the proper balance between freedom of expression and protection of reputation, proceedings might be stayed (abandoned) if it is apparent that the defamation proceedings will not achieve the legitimate purpose of protecting the claimant's reputation.

The starting point is the *presumption* in English law that the claimant's reputation has been damaged irrespective of whether or not that is true. In the court's opinion, if someone brought a defamation action and that person's reputation had suffered little or no damage, that might constitute an interference with freedom of expression. However, the correct way to deal with this type of situation is not to abandon the rule relating to presumption of damage but either challenge the claimant's resort to the jurisdiction or seek to strike out the action as an abuse of process. In this case, the latter option was chosen. It was judged that the five publications in this jurisdiction did not amount to a 'real and substantial tort'.

Elaine Chase v. News Group Newspapers Ltd [2002] EWCA Civ 1722

I have included this case not because of the substantive issues in it, but for an important statement of principle relating to the meaning of any alleged defamatory 'sting'. In *Lucas Box v. News Group Ltd [1986] 1 WLR 147*, the court had recognised that a defendant ought to set out in the statement of the case the defamatory meaning it is sought to prove. This could be at any one of three levels. Courts constantly refer to these three levels. A very clear statement on what the levels refer to is found in para. 45 of the judgment in the *Elaine Chase* case. Lord Justice Brooke said:

> *The sting of a libel may be capable of meaning that a claimant has in fact committed some serious act, such as murder. (1) Alternatively it may be suggested that the words mean that there are reasonable grounds to suspect that he/she has committed such an Act. (2) A third possibility is that they may mean that there are grounds for investigating whether he/she has been responsible for such an act. (3)*

These three levels are based on a statement by Lord Devlin in *Lewis v. Daily Telegraph [1964] AC 234*, p. 282:

> there could have been three different categories of justification – proof of the fact of an inquiry (Level 3), proof of reasonable grounds for it (Level 2) and proof of guilt (Level 1).

It will be important for you to mention these three levels when dealing with a defendant's response to a claim of defamation. The three levels were endorsed in April 2006 by Eady J in the case of *Fallon v. MGN Ltd [2006] EWHC 783 QB* (see para.1 of the judgment).

Financial Times & Others v. Interbrew SA [2002] EWCA Civ 274

Interbrew, one of the world's largest brewery companies, was in negotiation with South African Breweries about a possible rapprochement between the two organisations. Merchant bankers working for Interbrew produced a preliminary document. This document was copied and 'doctored' by a person unknown and sent to a number of reputable financial and business newspapers throughout Europe. Stories were published by the *Financial Times* and other UK newspapers. They had an immediate impact on the share price of South African Breweries and a corresponding negative impact on Interbrew's share price.

Interbrew brought proceedings seeking the return of the documentation in order to further its enquiries into the source of the leak.

Held

The Court of Appeal held that the High Court's order for disclosure was rightly made. The company had done everything possible to identify the source, but had failed. It was, said the court, entitled to receive assistance from the newspaper. As Lord Justice Sedley (para 55) said:

> The public interest in protecting the source of such a leak is in my judgment not sufficient to withstand the countervailing public interest in letting Interbrew seek justice in the courts against the source.

Clearly the court thought that a serious breach of trust had occurred and that, unless the source was identified, normal business transactions would be hindered because of the possibility of further breaches of confidence.

Please look at the implications of the House of Lords decision in *Norwich Pharmacal Co. v. Customs and Excise Commissioners [1974] AC 133*. This decision is the authority for the proposition that, if a person gets mixed up in the wrongdoing of others, the court has jurisdiction so as to facilitate it in helping the person who has been wronged by giving full information and disclosing the identity of the wrongdoers. Therefore, if the third party (in this case, the newspaper) receives information after a tort has been committed, then the court can order that the third party should assist the wronged organisation or person by disclosing any relevant information, including that which that will help to identify the miscreant. This principle has, over the years, been extended to occasions where there has been a breach of confidence that may not have amounted to a tortious act.

Gaddafi v. Telegraph Group [2000] EMLR 431

Saif Al Islam Gaddafi, the eldest son of Colonel Gaddafi, sued the *Sunday Telegraph* for alleging that he was attempting to breach economic sanctions in the aftermath of the Lockerbie air disaster.

The *Telegraph* was allowed to enter a plea of qualified privilege and state that its sources included a number of 'Western government security agents'.

Held

The court said that it would uphold the *Telegraph's* right to maintain confidentiality regarding the identities of its sources while still maintaining the qualified privilege defence. The judges simply needed to be satisfied that *sufficient information* had been disclosed to them to ascertain that they were credible and reliable sources.

Galloway MP v. Telegraph Group Ltd [2004] EWHC 2786 (QB)

The claimant in these libel proceedings was the Member of Parliament for Glasgow Kelvin. He was an active member of the Labour Party until he was expelled in October 2003. Thereafter, he became a founding member of a new political movement known as RESPECT. The movement was formed to campaign against the war in Iraq. Among its objectives is to challenge New Labour, bring an end to hostilities in Iraq and sever the special relationship with the USA.

In April 2003, *The Daily Telegraph* published a number of articles said to be based on documents found in badly damaged government offices in

Baghdad. The theme of the articles was that Galloway had been in the pay of Saddam's regime and was an apologist for that regime. The claimant attributed four 'natural and ordinary meanings' to the articles, which were that:

- the claimant was in the pay of Saddam Hussein and had secretly received at least £375,000 a year from his regime
- he had made very substantial secret profits, first, from Saddam Hussein and his regime by receiving money from the Oil for Food programme and, second, a percentage of the profit from a number of food contracts he had obtained from the Iraqi Ministry of Trade
- at a meeting in December 1999, he had asked an Iraqi intelligence agent for more money for himself
- he used the Mariam Appeal (a charity) as a front to conceal his secret commercial dealings with the Iraqi Intelligence Service and from these commercial dealings he sought to obtain very substantial sums of money for himself.

Unsurprisingly, Galloway sued for libel. *The Daily Telegraph* did not plead justification but relied on common law qualified privilege (*Reynolds* privilege) and fair comment as defences. The importance of the case is that it applies the ten *Reynolds* factors in order to decide whether or not *The Daily Telegraph* had passed the responsible journalism test.

Held

The judge, Eady J, found for Galloway and awarded him £150,000 in damages. The judge rejected the defence of qualified privilege for the following reasons.

1 Clearly – and this is a point that you must make to examiners – the story was of public interest, relating as it does to a serving British MP who, it is alleged, was in the pay of a regime against which the country went to war. However *The Daily Telegraph* did not pass the duty/interest test because, said the judge, it was not under any 'social or moral duty' to publish *at that time*. One of the *Reynolds* factors is whether or not the news would become stale. The judge felt that, as *The Daily Telegraph* had control of the story and the documents on which it was based, there was no need to rush to publication. To have waited a few days would have allowed Mr Galloway to give a more considered response than he had been hitherto permitted and *The Daily Telegraph* could have carried out some checks into the authenticity of the documents on which the story was based.

2 In answer to the question 'Had *The Daily Telegraph*'s journalism been 'responsible'?, the judge was clearly of the opinion that it had not. You should read this part of the judgment in order to see how the judge applied the *Reynolds* factors to answer this question. The judge felt that the tone of the coverage was 'dramatic and condemnatory'. In Lord Nicholls' words, 'this newspaper did not 'raise queries or call for an investigation', it chose to 'adopt allegations as statements of fact.' Even more significantly it went beyond the documents and drew its own conclusions. Another significant point that weighed heavily against *The Daily Telegraph* was the fact that no steps were taken to verify the information. The defendants claimed that they 'did not think they needed to do so, or that they were capable of carrying out any meaningful verification.'

3 As to the defence of fair comment, the judge was similarly unimpressed. Once he had established that *The Daily Telegraph* had turned accusations into statements of fact, it would have been difficult for him to conclude that all they were doing was expressing honest *opinions.* The judge therefore concluded that the newspaper had been making statements of fact and, as a result, could not rely on the defence of fair comment.

Comment

It is fair to say that *The Daily Telegraph,* to use Mr Galloway's word, was 'trounced'. The judge sent out a strong message to the newspaper industry that, in order to rely on common law qualified privilege, a newspaper must show that its journalism is essentially in accord with the *Reynolds* factors. If ever there was a case that demonstrated the truth of Sir Peter Stothard's words, (see p. 181), this is it. The decision is a shot across the bows of the industry to remind everyone that freedom of expression is crucial to the workings of a democracy, but it carries with it duties and responsibilities. The test is one of 'responsible journalism' and the sad part about this case is that *The Daily Telegraph* had a good story. If its staff had simply brought the existence of the documents into the public domain and perhaps called for an investigation rather than sensationalising the story and turning accusation into fact, then the judge, in all probability, would have upheld their defence of qualified privilege.

From a student's perspective – irrespective of whether you are an undergraduate or a trainee journalist – this is certainly a five-star case and should be studied by all who have more than a passing interest in media law.

GKR Karate v. Yorkshire Post [2000] 2 All ER 931

The owners of a free newspaper had accused the karate club of 'ripping off' its members. The court decided that it was appropriate, at the pre-trial stage, to consider whether or not the defence of qualified privilege should apply. Such a hearing would take a couple of days whereas a jury trial would last up to six weeks.

Held

The balancing exercise mandated in *Reynolds* came down in favour of the *Yorkshire Post*. The journalist had acted honestly and reported allegations made by an authoritative source. The local public said the court needed to be warned against dishonest door-to-door canvassing. The article was unsensational in tone. There were some inaccuracies and over-egging, but these did not outweigh the public interest in the free flow of information, or amount to malice.

Goodwin v. United Kingdom [1996] ECHR 16

The European Court of Human Rights held by 11 votes to 7 that the decision in the House of Lords had breached Goodwin's Article 10 rights. The Court emphasised that freedom of expression constituted one of the essential foundations of a democratic society and, in that context, safeguards afforded to the press were of particular importance. It was noted that, since the company was protected by an injunction, it need not go further and attempt to identify the source. The private interests of the company were not enough to outweigh the public interest in protection of sources.

Greene v. Associated Newspapers [2004] EWCA Civ 1462

Greene had applied for and been refused an injunction to prevent the *Mail on Sunday* from printing a story about her that she claimed was libellous. She appealed to the Court of Appeal against that decision. The *Mail on Sunday* had, the previous week, printed a story in which it asserted that Greene had become one of Cherie Blair's closest friends, helped the Blairs' to purchase a £3.6 million house and was a 'former business contact of convicted fraudster Peter Foster'. The article also contained e-mail communications, claimed to be from Greene to Foster, in which she agreed to act as a consultant for a new business venture and requested a fee of $15,000 to be paid directly into a bank account in the USA without the need for a 'UK-based invoice' – the implication being that she was trying to avoid paying tax. She denied sending the e-mail.

The *Mail on Sunday* was planning to publish another article the following Sunday and this was the one that she tried to stop by way of an injunction.

The judge made his decision only hours before the paper was due to print. In refusing to grant an injunction, the judge felt himself bound by the rule in *Bonnard v. Perryman [1891] 2 Ch 269*. The test in that case was that the claimant must demonstrate 'it is clear the alleged libel is untrue' in order to have any prospect of preventing publication (prior restraint). The judge concluded that, on the evidence laid before him, Greene had not made out her case to that 'high standard'. However, the judge made an order for a temporary injunction pending a decision from the Court of Appeal.

Held

The Court of Appeal found that *Bonnard v. Perryman* was good law and was compliant with European Human Rights law. The Court cited with approval the words of Lord Denning MR in *Fraser v. Evans [1969] 1 QB 349*, (para 47) to the effect that:

> The court will not restrain the publication of an article, even though it is defamatory, when the defendant says he intends to justify it or make fair comment on a matter of public interest ... the reason is the importance in the public interest that the truth should be out.

Brooke LJ then said the following as the rationale for the rule against prior restraint:

> In an action for defamation a court will not impose a prior restraint on publication unless it is clear that no defence will succeed at trial. This is partly due to the importance the court attaches to freedom of speech. It is partly because a judge must not usurp the constitutional function of the jury unless he is satisfied that there is no case to go to a jury. The rule is also partly founded on the pragmatic grounds that until there has been disclosure of documents and cross-examination at the trial a court cannot safely proceed on the basis that what the defendants wish to say is not true. And if it is or might be true the court has no business to stop them saying it.

In simple terms, then, if the article is proved to be libellous, then the claimant will have her remedy. She has not been deprived of it simply because the court refuses an injunction. If the allegations are true, then, as Lord Denning said, the truth must out.

Please note that the approach to prior restraint in *defamation* cases is decided by reference to the rule in *Bonnard v. Perryman,* whereas in cases of alleged breach of confidence, the decision in *Cream Holdings v. Banerjee* applies.

Henry v. BBC (No. 2) [2005] EWHC 2787 (QB)

An inquiry had been held by the Weston-super-Mare Health Authority into allegations that waiting list figures for admission to the hospital had been falsified. The regional BBC television programme Points West had broadcast a press conference held by a former employee who had named Mrs Henry as a manager who had instructed junior staff to manipulate the figures. Mrs Henry sued for defamation.

The BBC relied, in the first instance, on qualified privilege.

Held

The judge ruled that the issue of privilege should be tried separately from any other defence the BBC might wish to plead. Taking into account the ten *Reynolds* factors, the judge concluded that the defence failed. The public at that stage had no right to know the allegations made by the press conference. In addition, the BBC had not put the allegations to Mrs Henry and, therefore, the broadcast was not balanced.

Please note two things:

- the judge applied the ten factors in very much the same way that Eady J did in *Galloway*
- subsequently, the BBC pleaded the defence of justification and succeeded, (you should access this report for *Henry v. BBC (No 3) [2006] EWHC 386 (QB)* and add it to any notes you have made on the defence of justification).

HRH The Prince of Wales v. Associated Newspapers Ltd (No. 3) [2006] EWHC 522 (Ch)

The *Daily Mail* published extracts from a journal written by the Prince of Wales relating to the handover to the Chinese government of Hong Kong. The Prince claimed that the journal was not written for public consumption and had been circulated on a private and confidential basis to a limited number of friends. The information was leaked to the newspaper by a member of the Prince's staff. There were seven other journals written by the Prince in the possession of the newspaper. The Prince sued for breach of confidence and copyright.

Held

Summary judgment was entered in favour of the Prince in respect of the 'Hong Kong' journal only. The judge held that the Prince had a reasonable expectation of privacy concerning the journal.

In dealing with the newspaper's public interest defence, the court found that this was an aspect of his life that did not normally attract public scrutiny. The *Caroline* decision posed the question as to whether or not the published work/photograph would make a contribution to public debate. In this case, said the judge, the Hong Kong journal made little contribution to public debate.

Please note that the judge decided that any attempt to prevent the other seven journals from entering the public domain would have to be the subject of a full trial. At the time of writing, it is not known whether this will happen or the matter will be settled without further recourse to the courts.

This is an important judgment, following on as it does from the *McKennitt* decision. Blackburne J quotes Eady J with approval regarding the shifting balance between Article 8 and 10 protection.

Irvine v. Talk Sport Ltd [2003] EWCA Civ 423

In 1999, the management of Talk Radio UK decided to re-brand the station and concentrate on sports coverage. The station's name was changed. As part of the strategy, the company acquired the rights to cover prominent sporting events, including Formula One Grand Prix races. Seeking to generate advertising revenue, it employed a marketing company to get potential advertisers interested. A pack that included a leaflet purporting to show the well-known racing driver Eddie Irvine holding a small radio to his ear, on which the station's logo appeared, was sent to 1,000 advertisers. The image was of him but it had been doctored. In the original photograph, he was holding a mobile phone.

Irvine brought an action against TalkSport based on the facts that the use of his image was a misrepresentation, calculated to deceive the public into believing that he was endorsing TalkSport, and he had suffered loss and damage.

The defendants denied passing off. They claimed that their actions had been designed to amuse, not mislead.

It was held that Irvine's action succeeded. There are two things that need to be established to ensure success in a passing off action:

1 at the time of the acts complained of, the claimant had a significant reputation or goodwill

2 the actions of the defendants gave rise to a false message that would have been understood by a not insignificant section of the market that his goods had been endorsed, recommended or approved of by the claimant.

The judge accepted that 'Mr Irvine has a property right in his goodwill which he can protect from unlicensed appropriation consisting of a false claim or suggestion of endorsement of a third party's goods or business.'

The Court of Appeal awarded Irvine £25,000 in damages.

Jameel & Another v. Times Newspapers Ltd (2004) EWCA Civ 983

The Sunday Times published an article about Yousef Jameel, a Saudi billionaire, which said that there were reasonable grounds for suspecting that he had helped to fund the attack on the Twin Towers in New York and that he had associated with Osama Bin Laden.

The High Court held that he be permitted to sue *The Sunday Times* on the basis that the article bore only a level three meaning (see *Lucas-Box* case, p. 162). He appealed against that decision.

Held (Court of Appeal)

Jameel's appeal succeeded on the basis that an 'ordinary reasonable reader' could conclude that the words were capable of amounting to a level 2 meaning – that is, reasonable grounds for suspicion. The judge therefore had misdirected himself on this point and the appeal would be allowed.

Note that Jameel's family had purchased Hartwell, a British Car dealership, in 1990. The Court of Appeal held that to defame the *proprietor* was not to defame the *company*. To do that, any article had to suggest that the company was implicated in the alleged wrongdoing attributed to the individual. Nothing in this article 'came factually close to such a transmissible slur.' You should bear in mind that a company has a distinct legal personality and so it is not to be seen as an extension of its proprietor.

Jameel v Wall Street Journal Europe [2006] UKHL 44

The House of Lords had to deal with two legal issues. Both dealt with the law relating to defamation. The first issue and arguably the most important concerned the 'scope and application' of the *Reynolds* qualified privilege defence. The second point to require determination was whether or not a trading corporation needed to prove 'special damage' before being able to sue in defamation. The trial judge had rejected the newspaper's arguments on both the need for special damage and that it could rely on *Reynolds* privilege. The Court of Appeal ([2005] EWCA 74) had dismissed the newspaper's appeal on each ground.

The background facts were that in February 2002 the newspaper published an article entitled '**Saudi Officials Monitor Certain Bank Accounts.**' A sub-heading stated '**Focus Is On Those With Potential Terrorist Ties.**' The article told of requests that had been made by US law enforcement agencies to the Saudi Arabian Monetary Authority to monitor the bank accounts of some of the country's most prominent businessmen. A number of individuals and companies were named amongst them the 'Abdullatif Jamil Group of companies.' The article claimed that the purpose of this request was to ensure that those named were not 'wittingly or unwittingly' used for the channeling of funds to terrorist organisations (see Lord Bingham at paras. 1–4). At the trial, damages amounting to £30,000 and £10,000 were awarded against the newspaper.

Held (House of Lords)

The House allowed the newspaper's appeal on the issue of privilege and dismissed the appeal on the special damage issue.

Reynolds privilege

Do refer to all the speeches but focus in particular on the 'lead' speech delivered by Lord Hoffman. The decision can perhaps be explained by making the following points:

- to avoid confusion, the label *Reynolds Privilege* should no longer be used. From now on the defence should be referred to as the *Reynolds Public Interest Defence*. The reasoning is straightforward. If one looks at sections 14 and 15 and Schedule 1 of the Defamation Act 1996 it will be apparent that 'privilege' applies to journalists reporting on or from identifiable 'situations' or 'circumstances.' However, at the heart of the *Reynolds* defence is the story itself i.e. the content of the piece and it is that which is deemed to be protected when the media resorts to using the defence. Therefore the working assumption is that 'public interest' reports that contain defamatory statement will, subject to what is said below, be protected

- when deciding whether the publication is one that attracts the appellation 'public interest' the question was to ask whether the duty/interest test had been passed. Were the media under a social, moral or legal duty to publish and did the public have a corresponding interest in receiving the material? Although it may amount to the same assessment, the question henceforth will simply be for the judge to decide distinguishing 'the public interest' from what is 'of interest to the public.' Time will tell whether the existing terminology will continue to prove useful

- a key question for the judge is whether the alleged defamatory words are needed to be included in the piece. This will put the spotlight on the *editorial decision making*. This is something that had not featured in the application of the *Reynolds privilege*. Clearly any story can be told by extracting any potentially legally troublesome words. Whether it then becomes a story that will attract a readership is another matter. Therefore to focus on the editorial decision to allow a piece to be published with potentially defamatory content is a logical step to take

- you will recall that in *Bonnick v Morris* the Privy Council referred to *responsible journalism* as being the price journalists paid for the protection they received from this defence. The House reiterated that the final approach is to consider whether the media 'deserved' to be protected i.e. their Article 10 rights should prevail over the fundamental right of protection of reputation. Therefore the 10 Nicholls' factors will still remain at the heart of this defence. However, to meet the media's criticism of the way the defence had developed the factors will not be regarded as 'hurdles' to be overcome. Rather the factors will be considered in a more 'holistic' or 'liberal' sense which according to Lord Hoffman is the way they were originally intended to be applied.

Conclusion

The *Reynolds Public Interest* defence should now be applied as it was originally intended as recognition of the importance of the media's Article 10 rights. However, I'm sure the judges will still continue to watch carefully to determine whether journalistic standards start to slip. Lord Nicholls said in 1999 that 'The common law does not seek to set a higher standard than that of responsible journalism, a standard the media themselves espouse.' Lord Hope, in the current case, echoed these words when he said '"Responsible journalism" is a standard which everyone in the media and elsewhere can recognise.' We await the future with interest!

Presumption of damage.

By a 3:2 majority the House maintained the current legal position that no special damage needed to be proved in order for a company to sue for defamation. The following comments are a paraphrase of Lord Bingham's justification for preserving the rule:

- the good name of a company is valuable
- as a result this is ' ... a value that the law should protect.'
- the publication of a 'truly damaging' defamatory article about a corporation may not inevitably result in financial loss. This is because the corporation may promptly issue proceedings ' ... and the more diligent its pursuit of a claim, the less the chance that financial loss will actually accrue.'
- where it is shown that a corporation or company has been defamed but suffered no financial loss, any damages awarded should be 'kept strictly within modest bounds.'

Kaye v. Robertson & Sunday Sport [1991] F.S.R. 62

The television actor Gordon Kaye was seriously injured in a motoring accident. He had surgery and was recovering in the intensive care unit of a hospital.

A reporter and photographer working for the *Sunday Sport* newspaper used subterfuge to gain entry to the unit and purported to interview him and took photographs.

Held

Kaye's only remedy was a limited injunction for malicious falsehood, in order to prevent the newspaper from claiming that he had cooperated in the interview. The Court of Appeal regarded the intrusion as a 'monstrous invasion of privacy', but was virtually powerless at that time to grant a suitable remedy based on either confidence or privacy.

The outcome of this case led to changes in the Press Complaints Commission's Code of Practice. Clause 8 covers just such a situation, when the subject matter of a story is in hospital, and determines how the press should behave in such circumstances.

Lewis & Others v. King [2004] EWCA Civ 1329

Don King, the boxing promoter, brought an action for libel against a New York lawyer who had written articles for a Californian based boxing website. King claimed the articles alleged that he was anti-semitic. Despite the fact that all the parties were based in the USA the action was commenced in London. The trial judge accepted jurisdiction here based on the fact that King was well known within this jurisdiction and therefore had a reputation to defend in this country. The defendants appealed.

Held

The appeal was dismissed. Various principles were recognised by the Court of Appeal when approaching these 'forum shopping' cases. The first presumption was that the appropriate jurisdiction was where the tort was committed. Therefore was the libel 'published' in this country? The answer clearly was yes. Second, the claim for jurisdiction here will be stronger the greater the claimant's link with the jurisdiction. Third, a court would assume that the publisher would know the risks to be run when placing articles on the internet. Finally, the court would pay little or no attention to any 'juridical advantage' to be gained by the claimant because the internet encompassed numerous jurisdictions and the claimant must be free to choose the one where he believed his reputation was seriously under threat.

Loutchansky v. Times Newspapers [2001] EWCA Civ 1805

A Russian businessman brought an action against *The Times* over an article alleging that he was involved in money laundering and smuggling nuclear weapons. The allegations appeared in both the print and online editions.

The question was whether or not qualified privilege protected *The Times*.

Held

The Court of Appeal accepted that qualified privilege applied to the *print* edition because the duty/interest test was satisfied.

Turning to the *online* edition, it had been argued for *The Times* that qualified privilege should protect its online news archive. It said that it maintained on its website a publicly available archive of past issues 'as a service to the public at large.' The court held that qualified privilege did not apply to the archive. It reasoned that the archive material was 'stale news', so its publication could not rank in importance equally with the dissemination of contemporary material.

The point to note is that, where an archive contains potentially defamatory material, an appropriate notice should be attached, warning against treating it as the truth, and this measure would remove the sting from the material. Thus, the failure to attach any qualifications to the archive material over the years 'could not properly be described as responsible journalism.'

McKennitt v. Ash [2005] EWHC 3003 (QB)

Ash was a friend and occasional employee of Loreena McKennitt, a Canadian folk singer. Ash wrote a book about McKennitt's life, including disclosures about her relationships, feelings and emotions that McKennitt regarded as private. Ash refused to delete the passages to which her former friend objected. As a result, McKennitt took action against Ash for breach of confidence.

Held

The judge awarded McKennitt damages and an injunction preventing the publication of Ash's book. She was also granted a declaration that Ash had breached confidentiality.

This judgment is regarded as extremely important as it is the first English decision to fully embrace the principles enshrined in the *Caroline* case. Eady J spoke of courts being more willing to provide individuals with Article 8 protection against an intrusive media purporting to exercise its Article 10 rights. That protection, said the judge, was not merely available to celebrities but should also be more widely available. The judges would place greater emphasis on scrutinising any claim by the media to be acting in the public interest when revealing personal information, especially where there was a clear commercial interest from the media's perspective. He also added that, even when information published about someone is untrue, the claimant could be protected under Article 8, otherwise, in revealing which was true or untrue, the person would be losing whatever privacy protection the law offered.

McManus & Others v. Beckham [2002] EWCA Civ 939

The claimants alleged that the defendant came into their shop and, in a 'rude, loud and unreasonable way', advised the customers present that the autograph on a photograph of her husband, David, was a fake. It was also alleged that the defendant said things to the effect that the claimants habitually sold memorabilia with fake autographs and she was advising customers not to buy them. The incident received massive press coverage and, as a result, there had been a dramatic downturn in their business.

The newspapers concerned included the *Daily Mirror, The People, News of the World* and the *Sunday Mirror,* and some also gave details of the incident on their websites.

The point of law raised by appeal was whether or not the claimants were entitled to rely on the press coverage to establish the loss that they had suffered.

The judge held that the newspaper article did not repeat the whole of the 'sting', only part. Second, the publication resulted from the independent acts of a third party, for which the defendant was not responsible. Third, he held that the claimants could not prove that a 'particular publisher' would repeat her words to the media.

The claimants appealed.

Held (allowing the appeal)

The legal principle (per Laws LJ) was that it had to be demonstrated the defendant *foresaw* that the further publication would *probably* take place or the defendant (or a reasonable person in her position) should have also foreseen and that, because of the likelihood of publication, in consequence, damage to the claimant would ensue.

Lord Justice Waller put it this way:

> *If a defendant is actually aware (1) that what she says or does is likely to be reported, and (2) that if she slanders someone that slander is likely to be repeated in whole or in part, there is no injustice in her being held responsible for the damage that the slander causes via that publication.*

The court also held that the judge's refusal to accept that the newspapers did not 'repeat the slander' because only part of the 'sting' was published was 'simply wrong.'

Mersey Care NHS Trust v. Ackroyd [2006] EWHC 107 (QB)

The question for the court was whether or not it should order Robin Ackroyd, a journalist, to disclose the name of his source at Ashworth High Security Hospital. It will be remembered that the source revealed medical records pertaining to Ian Brady, the Moors Murderer. The case was heard some seven years after the information was passed to him and, ultimately, published by the *Daily Mirror*.

Held

The hospital was seeking redress against a source who may no longer work at the hospital. Indeed he or she may not still be alive. In all probability, the hospital would never achieve redress, even if the name was revealed.

In refusing to make the order sought by the hospital, the judge considered that the journalist had acted responsibly. The case should *not* be taken as authority that medical records are to be treated as anything other than confidential and will be protected by the courts. Forcing the journalist to reveal the name of his source would not be proportionate to the benefit to be gained from the exercise.

Milne v. Express Newspapers PLC [2004] EWCA Civ 664 [2004] EMLR 24

The claimant had not accepted an offer to make amends and wanted to proceed to trial by jury. In order to do so under the terms of the Defamation Act 1996, he had to seek to establish that the defendants 'knew or had reason to believe that the statement complained of ... was both false and defamatory of him' (section 4(3)).

Held

The judge at first instance and the Court of Appeal found that he could not establish that, at the very least, the defendants had been reckless per Lord Diplock in *Horrocks v. Lowe [1975] AC 135*. His claim failed because the fact of an offer to make amends is a defence to defamation proceedings, unless the claimant can successfully rely on section 4(3).

Read paras 13 and 14 of the report as there is an excellent account there of the background to and purpose of the offer of amends procedure.

Nail v. News Group Newspapers & Others [2004] EWCA Civ 1708

The appellant in this case is a well-known television actor and musician. The *News of the World* published an article entitled, 'Auf Wiedersehen Jimmy's Secret Bondage Orgies'. The title is a fair representation of the content. There was a second action against Geraint Jones, the author of a book entitled *Nailed: The Biography of Jimmy Nail* (Harper Collins, 1998). Nail brought defamation actions against each party.

In each action, there were offers to make amends, which were accepted. After negotiation, agreed apologies were published. The final matter was agreed compensation. The claimant suggested somewhere in the range of £70,000–£100,000. The judge awarded £30,000, which he described as 'by modern standards still substantial.' The defendants had already paid this amount into court and therefore Nail was saddled with the legal costs, estimated at over £200,000. If the amount awarded by the judge had been higher than that paid into court, then he would not have had the costs awarded against him. He appealed on the amount of damages.

Held

The Court of Appeal could find no ground for coming to the conclusion that the trial judge had been wrong in his assessment of the damages. The judge said the court had given 'proper and full consideration to all relevant factors and reached a balanced conclusion.' Note the following point of principle from May LJ:

> I would reject entirely any idea that there might be a conventional or standard percentage discount when an offer to make amends has been accepted and an agreed apology published. Each case will be different and require individual consideration.

Norman v. Future Publishing Ltd [1999] EMLR 325

A profile of the opera singer Jessye Norman appeared in *Classic CD* magazine. In the course of the article, the journalist referred to Norman's 'statuesque physique' and made an observation to the effect that, on one occasion, she became trapped in swing doors and, being told to turn sideways in order to release herself, replied, 'Honey, I ain't got no sideways.'

She brought defamation proceedings over the way the magazine article had portrayed her use of language. She alleged the *natural and ordinary* meaning was that she had a mode of speech that was vulgar and undignified and/or conformed to a degrading racial stereotype. In addition, she maintained that it suggested she was guilty of patronising mockery of the modes of speech stereotypically associated with certain groups or classes of black Americans.

Held

The Court of Appeal held that, in the context of the article taken as a whole, it was not capable of bearing the meaning alleged. The article was found to be extremely complimentary of Norman, portraying her as a person of high standing and impeccable dignity – the very reverse of vulgar.

Peck v. United Kingdom [2003] ECHR 44

The applicant suffered from depression. One evening he walked down the High street in Brentwood with a knife in his hands and attempted to commit suicide by cutting his wrists. His actions were caught on CCTV owned by Brentwood Council. Some time later the footage appeared on regional television and was released, subject to conditions, to the BBC. One of the conditions was that no one was to be identified from the footage. However, part of the footage was used to trail a BBC series and friends of the applicant identified him. He brought an action against the UK government claiming that English law was deficient in that it did not provide him with an adequate remedy for breach of his privacy.

Held

The European Court of Human Rights decided in the applicant's favour and found that English law failed to provide suitable remedies in respect of breaches of his Article 8 rights. The case must now be read in light of the developments in English law post *Caroline* and *Campbell* and the important decisions of *McKennitt v. Ash* and *Prince Charles*. Given the decision in Peck was delivered early in 2003 the case could be seen as the precursor for the developments in privacy law that have occurred subsequently. It is worth dipping into the report for the review of privacy/confidentially laws undertaken by the court in the early years of the new millennium.

Prince Albert v. Strange [1849] 64 ER 293

The defendant was a publisher. He had purchased private etchings of the Queen's family and was selling them across London. It transpired that the etchings had come from a publishing house in Windsor, to which the Royal family occasionally sent their photographic plates to be printed. A member of staff had taken additional copies for private gain. The Prince sought an injunction preventing the sale of the copies.

Held

The injunction was granted. It will be noted that Strange was a 'third party' in the sense that there was no contractual relationship between him and the Prince. However, the court was adamant that the etchings had been obtained as a result of a breach of trust and Strange was aware of that fact. As Lord Hoffman (para 45) commented in the *Campbell* case:

> *It was not essential that the information should concern the Prince's family life or be in any other way personal. Any confidential information would have done. Nor was it intended that the defendant should have intended widespread publication. Communication to a single unauthorised person would have been enough. Many of the cases on breach of confidence are concerned with the communication of commercially valuable information to trade rivals and not with anything that could be described as a violation of privacy.*

Reynolds v. Times Newspapers Ltd [1999] UKHL 45

Reynolds was a former Prime Minister of Ireland who sued *The Sunday Times* after the newspaper had published an article in its English mainland edition accusing him of misleading Parliament and deceit in relation to coalition cabinet colleagues. Interestingly, the Irish edition of the same newspaper did not repeat the allegations.

The House of Lords heard the case after the Human Rights Act went on to the statute book, but before it came into force on 2 October 2000.

The newspaper defended the case on the basis that it was not to be liable for a defamatory statement made in the course of political discussion and published in good faith. In other words, the common law defence of qualified privilege.

Held

The House of Lords was not prepared to recognise a 'generic qualified privilege', in the sense that *all* political communications would not attract liability if libellous, without proof that the newspaper acted *recklessly* or in bad faith.

The House recognised that, with the passing of the Human Rights Act, freedom of expression was a fundamental right and was to be given every support by the judiciary. As Lord Nicholls (at page 53) said:

> To be justified, any curtailment of freedom of expression must be convincingly established by a compelling countervailing consideration, and the means employed must be proportionate to the end sought to be achieved.

The House went on to decide that a defendant could plead qualified privilege at common law regarding any communication, provided it passed the duty/interest test. Essentially, this is a public interest test based on the idea that the newspaper is under a duty to publish and the readership has a corresponding interest in receiving the information. This was quite clearly a public interest story because of the impact Reynold's resignation would have on the Northern Ireland peace process. As such, the English readership had an interest in receiving the information. The duty/interest test was therefore passed.

However, that wasn't enough to win the case for *The Sunday Times*. Had the story been published with reasonable care and balance? The House decided that it had not. The Law Lords found that Reynolds had not been given sufficient opportunity to respond to the allegation and the newspaper had omitted altogether any reference to his resignation speech to the Irish Parliament.

The name of this case has become a byword for assessing whether or not a newspaper or journalist has behaved responsibly. If the newspaper or journalist has, then, providing the duty/interest test is passed, then freedom of expression will take precedence over protection of reputation.

In what has become a landmark speech, Lord Nicholls offered up ten factors that a court should take into account when assessing the conduct of any newspaper. You should learn, or at least understand, the genesis of these factors.

1 The seriousness of the allegation. The more serious the charge, the more the public is misinformed and the individual harmed if the allegation is *not* true.

2 The nature of the information and the extent to which the matter is one of public concern.

3 The source of the information. Is the source reliable? Do you know the source? Some sources have their own personal axes to grind.

4 The steps taken to verify the information.

5 The status of the information. The allegation may already have been subject to an investigation, which commands respect. In other words, don't ignore official reports. (See *Selistö v. Finland,* for example.)

6 The urgency of the matter. News is very often a perishable commodity.

7 Has comment been sought from the claimant? Note, though, an approach to the claimant will not always be necessary.

8 Did the article contain the gist of the claimant's side of the story?

9 The tone of the article. A paper can raise queries or call for an investigation. It need not (should not?) adopt allegations as statements of fact.

10 The circumstances of the publication, including the timing.

If you are a trainee journalist, then you would do well to note the words of Sir Peter Stothard, the former editor of *The Times* and now Editor of *The Times Literary Supplement,* when he said, in February 2004:

> My recommendation is that every practising journalist should get to grips with Reynolds and understand it. It should be the one-page training manual available to all. Everything about the Nicholls tests is true. It still astonishes me how few people know about them. Every editor should apply them and every journalist should know about them.

Roberts & Another v. Gable & Another [2006] EWHC 1025 (QB)

The *Searchlight* magazine had published an article in which it was alleged that there was 'feuding' between various factions of the British National Party. The claimants, both members of the BNP, claimed that the articles made serious allegations about their honesty and said they were willing to use violence against other BNP members.

The magazine pleaded *Reynolds* privilege. The preliminary question was whether or not the article was protected by common law qualified privilege.

Held

The court found that it was applying the reportage principle. The article clearly passed the duty/interest test because it concerned the activities of a political party. Citizens have an interest in hearing or reading such information as the party in question would contest elections in the particular area. There was no evidence that the magazine was attempting to take sides and, therefore, the report fell under the reportage principle. The reasonable reader or viewer would, the judge said, be more concerned to know about the internal disputes than whether or not the information was strictly correct.

Please note that, although this is a common law qualified privilege case, it was decided on the reportage principle espoused in the case of *Al-Fagih v. HH Saudi Research and Marketing (UK) Ltd [2002] EMLR 215*. On the issue of reportage, please see the *Galloway v. Telegraph* decision at first instance.

Re. S (FC) (a Child) (Appellant) [2004] UKHL 47

In this case, a mother had been charged with the murder of her son. A request was made to a judge in the Family Division of the High Court that she should not be identified at her trial in order to protect the privacy of her other son, who was not involved in the proceedings. At the time of the proceedings he was aged eight.

The press wished to report the case and use photographs of the woman, her husband and the victim. The request was refused and the decision supported by the Court of Appeal.

Held (dismissing the appeal)

An appeal made to the House of Lords was dismissed. The decision revolved around the interplay between Articles 10 and 8 of the European Convention on Human Rights. The House made four important statements of principle:

- neither Article has precedence over the other
- when the Articles are in conflict, there must be a detailed examination of the 'comparative importance of the specific rights being claimed'
- the judiciary must take into account the justifications for interfering with or restricting each right
- the proportionality test must be applied and this was referred to as 'the ultimate balancing test'.

The House reaffirmed the 'ordinary rule' – that the press may report 'everything that takes place in a criminal court' – and that this rule could only be displaced by 'unusual or exceptional circumstances'. Clearly section 39 of the Children and Young Persons Act did not apply because this child was not a 'young person concerned in the *proceedings.*'

The House pointed out that there are no legal provisions other than injunctions that can protect children who are not party to the proceedings. However, the House strongly supported the right of the press, at both national and local levels, to report what was, in all likelihood, going to be a 'sensational' trial. Otherwise, as Lord Steyn said, public discussion of criminal justice would be 'seriously impoverished'.

Secretary of State for Defence v. Guardian Newspapers [1984] 3 All ER 601

The Ministry of Defence prepared a secret memorandum regarding the deployment of Cruise missiles. Copies were sent to the Prime Minister and six senior cabinet colleagues. An unknown informant leaked a photocopy to *The Guardian* newspaper. The Crown requested the return of the photocopied document in an attempt to identify the source. *The Guardian* declined the invitation because it feared that the source would then be identified. It claimed protection under section 10. The Crown argued, inter alia, that it was in the interests of national security that the defaulting Crown servant be identified.

Held

By a 3:2 majority, the House of Lords found in favour of the Crown. The majority seemed persuaded by the fact that national security *in the future* might be jeopardised if the informant was not identified. Any further leaking might have more devastating consequences for national security.

The document was subsequently handed over and the informant, Sarah Tisdall, a Foreign Office clerk, was imprisoned for six months for breaching the Official Secrets Act.

Theakston v. MGN Ltd [2002] EWHC 137 (QB)

The claimant is a television personality who, at the time, presented the BBC's *Top of the Pops* programme and also had a weekly show on Radio 1.

After an evening drinking with three friends, he visited a Mayfair brothel where one or more of the customers or the prostitutes took photographs of him in compromising positions. The photographs and story ended up with the *Sunday People* and it proposed to publish. There was a hint that the photographs could have been taken for the purpose of blackmail, but it is not suggested the *Sunday People* was in any way associated with the taking or any unlawful use of the photographs.

Theakston sought an injunction preventing the *Sunday People* from publishing on the grounds of breach of confidentiality and of his right to privacy under Article 8 and the PCC's Code of Practice.

Held

Theakston succeeded in obtaining an injunction in relation to the photographs, but not the story. The reasoning regarding the article follows the line taken by Lord Denning in *Woodward v. Hutchins [1977] 1 WLR 760,* which has since also been supported by the House of Lords in the *Campbell* case in 2004.

As Ouseley J said in 2002, (para 48) Theakston had over the years courted publicity by projecting an image of being:

> a man physically and sexually attractive to many women. He has not objected to those with whom he had had sexual relations discussing those relations both in general and in more explicit and in more intimate detail ... He has courted publicity of that sort and not complained of it when, hitherto, it has been largely favourable to him ... the claimant cannot complain if the publicity given to his sexual activities is less favourable in this instance.

In other words, the truth must out and, under Article 10, the media has every right to put the information into the public domain.

However, regarding the photographs, the judge took a different view. The photographs were not taken with the claimant's consent. The authorities cited to the judge persuaded him to conclude that the courts have consistently recognised that photographs can be particularly intrusive and (para 78):

> have showed a high degree of willingness to prevent publication of photographs taken without the consent of the person photographed but which the photographer or someone else sought to exploit and publish.

The judge could see no public interest in their public publication. He expressed it this way, taking into account the European Convention rights (para 79):

> *I considered that the right to freedom of expression by publication of such photographs was outweighed by the peculiar degree of intrusion into the integrity of the Claimant's personality that their publication would entail.*

Please bear this case in mind when considering the implications of the *Caroline* decision. Is there any 'real' distinction between the cases in terms of reasoning? Can it be said that Princess Caroline and Theakston were both in 'public places' engaged in 'everyday activities' in which there was no public interest to warrant publication? Caroline wished to play tennis with her future husband and go riding. Theakston preferred to engage in sexual relations with consenting adults. Each court decided that there was no public interest in publishing photographs of these activities.

Wainwright & Another v. Home Office [2003] UKHL 53

On a visit to Armley Jail in Leeds, Wainwright and her son were strip searched. It was admitted that the procedure used did not comply with internal rules. Her son was severely embarrassed and suffered post-traumatic stress disorder. Wainwright herself suffered emotional distress.

They commenced an action against the Home Office.

The judge concluded that their privacy had been infringed. The Court of Appeal disagreed. In such a situation, the court said, there had been no breach of confidentiality, but would not go further and recognise a right to sue for breach of privacy.

Held (dismissing the appeal)

An appeal to the House of Lords was dismissed. The House acknowledged that the Court of Appeal thought it was time for parliamentary intervention, but was not prepared to countenance the creation of a general tort of privacy via the Judicial Committee of the House of Lords. Lord Hoffman was concerned about the creation of a *general* right of privacy as opposed to recognising that remedies might become available in certain defined situations. So, taking the example of *Peck v. United Kingdom* (see above), a remedy could (and perhaps should) be created that would deal with the sensitivity issues connected with the use of CCTV film. The Peck case was not deemed to be an authority for the general proposition that the UK should create a new tort for the invasion of privacy.

NB See now the decision of the European Court of Human Rights in *Wainwright v. United kingdom [2006] ECHR 807.*

X Ltd & Others v. Morgan Grampian Ltd [1990] 2 All ER 1

A copy of a confidential and commercially sensitive business plan was stolen from the plaintiff's premises. The following day, William Goodwin, a trainee journalist working for *The Engineer* magazine, took a telephone call from an unnamed source who released the information to him. He decided to write an article about the plaintiffs and telephoned them and their bankers to check certain details. They, in turn, sought and obtained an ex parte injunction restraining publication and applied under section 10 for the journalist to reveal the source of the information. The plaintiffs believed that the identity of the source could be discovered if they could have access to the journalist's notes of the telephone conversation he had with the source.

Held [House of Lords]

The House, inevitably, had to engage in a balancing exercise. The protection of a source, it said, is 'of high importance'. Nothing less than *necessity* would override the protection offered by section 10. Whether or not it was necessary in this case would be determined by reference to 'another matter of high public importance' – namely the four matters of public interest listed in section 10.

The House held that it was in the interests of justice that people should be able to exercise legal rights and 'protect themselves from serious legal wrongs regardless of whether or not resort to legal proceedings in a court of law was necessary to attain those objectives.'

In this case, the disclosure of the stolen information posed a serious threat to the plaintiff's business and there had been a 'gross breach of confidentiality'. In turn, this had not been counterbalanced by any legitimate interest that publication of the information was calculated to serve.

As a result, the House ordered that the journalist's notes be released.

This case should be read together with its sequel in the European Court of Human Rights decision.

4.5

contempt of court: prejudicial reporting

Mr Justice Moses, the judge at the Soham murder trial of Ian Huntley and Maxine Carr, told the media (April 2003):

> *The detection and suppression of crime depends to an important degree on a fair trial with safe verdicts. The press plays its part in that fairness by ensuring balanced and fair reporting. I cannot imagine that any journalist wants to face the families and friends of the victims, whose interests they so loudly seek to defend, and confess that their work, their articles, their stories, their photographs have prevented a trial taking place at all or continuing. In short the important right of the press to report on public trials carries with it a responsibility to protect fairness of a trial not just for the defendants but for the victims, their families and the community.*

Conclusion

I think that these words provide a fitting reminder that the media has important rights and the attributes of a free press are vital to a thriving, democratic society. However, with those rights come responsibilities and, ultimately, it is for an independent judiciary to determine whether or not the media have complied with those responsibilities.

index